The Art of
Focused Conversation
for Schools

Over 100 Ways to Guide Clear Thinking
and Promote Learning

The Art of
Focused Conversation
for Schools

Over 100 Ways to Guide Clear Thinking
and Promote Learning

JO NELSON

NEW SOCIETY PUBLISHERS

ICA
CANADA
The Canadian Institute of Cultural Affairs

Cataloguing in Publication Data:
A catalog record for this publication is available from the National Library of Canada.

Editors: Ronnie Seagren and Brian Griffith.
Design and layout: Ilona Staples.

Printed in Canada on acid-free, partially recycled (20 percent post-consumer) paper using soy-based inks by Transcontinental/Best Book Manufacturers.

New Society Publishers acknowledges the financial support of the Government of Canada through the Book Publishing Industry Development Program (BPIDP) for our publishing activities, and the assistance of the Province of British Columbia through the British Columbia Arts Council.

Paperback ISBN: 0-86571-435-5

Inquiries regarding requests to reprint all or part of *The Art of Focused Conversation for Schools: Over 100 Ways to Guide Clear Thinking and Promote Learning* should be addressed to New Society Publishers at the address below.

To order directly from the publishers, please add $4.00 shipping to the price of the first copy, and $1.00 for each additional copy (plus GST in Canada). Send check or money order to:

New Society Publishers
P.O. Box 189, Gabriola Island, BC, Canada V0R 1X0

New Society Publishers aims to publish books for fundamental social change through nonviolent action. We focus especially on sustainable living, progressive leadership, and educational and parenting resources. Our full list of books can be browsed on the worldwide web at: http://www.newsociety.com

Copublished by

NEW SOCIETY PUBLISHERS
www.newsociety.com

The Canadian Institute of Cultural Affairs (ICA Canada)
579 Kingston Road, Toronto, ON Canada M4E 1R3

Table of Contents

Part IV **Appendices**

Acknowledgements

One of my insights from the writing of this book is the huge benefit of incorporating the wisdom of a diverse group of people for both learning and the communication of knowledge. I would like to thank all of those who influenced this book.

My mother, Luella Reese, who modeled intentional teaching from before I can remember.

My father, Donald Reese, who instilled the habit of thoughtful dialogue in our family.

My husband Wayne Nelson, who continues to challenge me to think clearly and deeply.

Our sons, Aaron and Timothy Nelson, who taught me a lot about how children learn, and gave me the opportunity to see schools from the parent's perspective.

My brother and his wife, David and Linda Zahrt, who originally introduced me to ICA and its methods.

Those who taught me ICA's Imaginal Education tools: Lidoña Wagner, Marilyn Oyler, Kaze Gadway, Karen Snyder Troxel, Jim Wiegel, Jean Long, Iris Boivin, Jeanette Stanfield, and Keith Packard, among others.

Pat DeSpain, who actively mentored me through my despair in my first year of teaching.

Schools and faculty I've taught with, from whom many of the stories of the book are drawn: Charles Drew Elementary, Washington, DC; Manley Upper Grade Center, Chicago; Roosevelt and Harrison Elementary Schools in Peoria, Illinois; Bayad Village Preschool, Bayad al Arab, Beni Suef, Egypt; Ijede Village Preschool, Ijede, Lagos State,

Nigeria; Middle School, Carrizo Springs, Texas; Save the Children Preschool, Murrin Bridge, NSW, Australia; The schools in Lake Cargelligo, NSW, Australia; Woburn Lawn School, Ness Castle, Jamaica.

School boards in Canada with whom I have worked as a facilitator and trainer, particularly Durham and Durham Separate boards, Thames Valley, Upper Grand, Peel, and Dawson Creek.

The staff of ICA Associates, Inc. with whom I teach facilitation, who supported my efforts each in their own unique way, and who added incredible strength to the book with their serious editing: Brian Stanfield, Jeanette Stanfield, Wayne Nelson, Duncan Holmes, Bill Staples, Ilona Staples, John Miller, Janis Clennett, Christine Wong, Sheighlah Hickey, Waheeda Rosanally, Rick Sterling, Renaud Houzeau De Lehaie, Marie-Noelle Houzeau De Lehaie.

The board of ICA Canada, particularly Judy Harvie, the Chair, for their encouragement.

The more than forty people who shared conversations they had designed for schools, who are named in Appendix 1.

And finally, Ronnie Seagren and Brian Griffith, for their incisive editing.

Part I

Theory

CHAPTER 1

The Importance of Focused Conversation for Schools

Thinking, questioning and imagining are the tools of human consciousness, the things that make us different from animals or machines. These are the tools of initiative; the initiative responsible individuals need in order to participate and to construct their lives.

John Ralston Saul

Teacher staff rooms all over the world are buzzing with frustrated stories and controversial questions about teaching — Why don't kids learn? Why can't they seem to perform higher order thinking? Why aren't the kids motivated to learn what we want them to learn? Why can't they learn to work or get along with others?

And then there are the frustrations about time-consuming lesson plans, endless staff meetings with little results, difficulties with parents, and misunderstandings with other staff. Parents, students, and administrators struggle with similar questions.

The pressures upon educators to teach more to a wider range and number of students, with decreasing resources and supports, make it urgent to find tools to answer these questions.

Surely there must be a process that can help people achieve clear and in-depth thinking, whether it is in the classroom, the staff meeting, the school council, or even in one-on-one conversations. There must be a way to facilitate interaction among students, parents and teachers on a topic in such a way to lead to useful learning.

And there is. When I first started teaching school in 1970, a naive young farm woman in an inner-city classroom, I was given a practical model for creating and guiding conversations. Over the past 30 years I have found this method invaluable for facilitating learning of children and adults, for making learning meaningful in real life, for strengthening and deepening communication, and for solving problems both alone and with groups. It has also proved invaluable for giving students a logical framework to structure their own thinking.

This method has variously been called the "art form method", the "discussion method", the "Focused Conversation method", and "O-R-I-D" for its four levels. At its simplest, the method moves through four levels of thinking:

Objective: dealing with data and sensory observation,

Reflective: related to personal reactions and associations,

Interpretive: about meaning, significance and implications, and

Decisional: concerned with resolution.

It was developed through four decades of work by the Institute of Cultural Affairs, based on research and also on observations of how people process information.

This book is written with the purpose of sharing the Focused Conversation method with teachers, administrators, parents, and students as a tool to answer their questions.

The next paragraphs illustrate the range of functions this method can serve in a school setting. Its use has the potential to:

a) extend thinking and learning capacity,

b) make learning meaningful,

c) make communication in groups effective,

d) help prevent and solve problems, and

e) strengthen the effectiveness of evaluation.

A. Extending Thinking and Learning Capacity

Facilitating the Capacity to Think Abstractly

Many times, when as a teacher, I had children read a story, I asked them immediately, "What is the story about?" Children always responded with very superficial answers, such as "It's about two children and their dog." It was not until I became familiar with the Focused Conversation method that I realized it didn't have to be this way.

One summer nearly 30 years ago, I was teaching a preschool group at a summer camp. I had the four-year-olds recite the familiar nursery rhyme, "Little Miss Muffet". Then we had a brief conversation on the rhyme, roughly as follows:

Objective Questions

"What words don't you understand?" (tuffet, curds and whey, which I explained)

"Who were the characters?" (Little Miss Muffet, the spider)

"What happened first? Then...Then...?"

"What did Miss Muffet do when she was frightened?"

Reflective Questions

"Where have you experienced something like this?" (One child said that his mother made him eat cottage cheese, and he hated it. Several children had stories of scary surprises, and their reactions.)

Interpretive Questions

Then I asked, "What is this story all about?"

One little girl thought for a second, then her eyes lit up. "This is about...when you get scared, you can decide if you're going to run away, or not!"

Decisional Questions

She finished up with "Next time I will decide by myself what to do!"

I was astounded. This tiny child had seen far below the surface of this rhyme to a meaning that had relevance to her own life. Her capacity to abstract meaning, or to access a higher level of thinking, was empowered by the step-by-step thinking process of the Focused Conversation method.

This method facilitates learning, as it starts with the obvious and most easily accessed information and moves step by step through to higher levels of thinking, thus extending students' capacity to think abstractly.

Teaching Clear Thinking

The Focused Conversation method can be taught to students as a tool for analytical and creative thinking.

A teacher in a grade 7 class creates a simple poster of the four steps and puts it up in the classroom.

Although a simple poster cannot really teach the process well, it communicates the basic structure of thought which is reinforced over and over again in a variety of class activities.

Students are first asked to write book reports using the formula, which is spelled out in more detail in specific questions on a form. Instructions for cooperative learning projects are written in this format. As each lesson finishes, the teacher uses the format to reflect on what was learned.

At the end of each day, the class writes journal entries using the format. By the end of the year, essays and science projects are revealing the same format, with sound and thought-provoking results.

Students who have a model for clear thinking write more thoughtful papers. They take their learning to its implications and application. They have a tool for problem solving in real life. The conversation method provides a powerful tool for clear thinking and its expression.

A Logical Structure for Presentations

A high school teacher explains the safety rules for shop class.

Objective Level: He describes an accident he has seen using power tools,

Reflective Level: He emphasizes what worries him.

Interpretive Level: He says a few sentences about what behavior caused the accident.

Decisional Level: He then puts out the safety rules he has drawn up and will insist be demonstrated in class.

Chances are high that the class will understand the thinking behind the rules, reach a similar interpretation, and follow the rules.

Not everything can be taught with open-ended questions. Often there is information and wisdom that a teacher has to share with students. The logical structure of the four-level process can be used to make a presentation, giving facts first, then associations and feelings, then the significance or meaning of this information, then conclusions, just as the shop teacher did in the illustration. This provides a window into the thought process of the teacher, communicating clearly how the conclusions are reached. This makes it possible for students to have a more complete understanding of the presentation.

B. Making Learning Meaningful

A Structure for Lesson Planning which Includes Application

A fifth grade science teacher provides students with materials and a period of time during class to experiment with building bridges in small groups, then some weights to test the strength of the constructions.

Objective Level: First they draw and graph their results.

Reflective Level: In the next part of the lesson, the students reflect on what they did and its effects.

Interpretive Level: In the third part, students compare their bridge designs with photos or architectural drawings of real bridges and structures to extract the effective design principles.

Decisional Level: Finally, students construct a small climbing structure for the playground.

The four steps provide a structure for lesson planning, allowing the presentation of information to be processed and applied before the end of the lesson. As students act upon their learnings, they see the lesson's relevance to real life. Generally, they are motivated to continue learning.

Dealing with Missed Information and Strengthening Communication

A chemistry teacher begins class with a quick but fascinating demonstration. Several chemicals are mixed together and the series of reactions ends in a cloud of orange smoke. The teacher asks the following questions.

>*Objective Level:* "What just happened?" Some students have noticed some things, some others. Together they reconstruct the events in the order in which they happened.

>*Reflective Level:* "Where have you seen something like this before?" One student, usually sleepy, tells a dramatic story of an explosion he caused with a chemistry set as a child. Everyone laughs. Another tells a story from a documentary on movie special effects.

>*Interpretive Level:* "Why do you think this happened? What are possible explanations? Which explanation makes most sense to you? What do you think is the underlying principle here? How does this compare with the textbook explanation?" Students try out theories, discuss them animatedly, then compare them with the events that happened and their text.

>*Decisional Level:* "How might this principle be used in industry?" This provokes some creative applications and provides a spin-off to the next lesson.

As a process for discussions, using the Focused Conversation method strengthens communication. It deals with missed understandings as they arise, whether with students, with parents, or with staff. A simple recall question, "What steps did we just do?" allows students to be filled in on things they missed, without embarrassment. A structured conversation allows more students to participate, as the different levels draw out different student strengths and learning capacities. One student may have vivid associations or strong reactions, while another is fascinated with moral implications. As arguing is replaced with respectful listening to the insights of others, less assertive students find it easier to communicate their ideas publicly.

C. Making Communication in Meetings and Group Work Effective

Building Shared Understanding and Respect

At a school in rural Australia, there was much grumbling by the white teachers about the behavior of Aboriginal kids. When the teachers and some parents sat down together to discuss the problem, they started with observations.

>*Objective Level:* A teacher said, "When you speak to a child, he doesn't look at you, even when you ask him to."

>*Reflective Level:* Then parents and teachers shared their reactions. Teachers felt rebuffed when children didn't look at them, and often grew angry. Parents

responded that they expected this behavior from the children, and were baffled by the teachers' anger.

Interpretive Level: As they explored the patterns behind these reactions, the teachers discovered that in Aboriginal culture, it is a sign of respect to look down when an elder person is speaking to you, because to look into someone's eyes is to violate their privacy. Parents discovered that people of European descent looked into each other's eyes to demonstrate attention, and experienced looking away as disrespect.

Decisional Level: The next step was to act upon ways to bridge the cultural gap. The misunderstandings were resolved in a respectful way that allowed further dialogue.

As people move together step by step to build shared understanding at a deeper and deeper level, respect and consensus begin to emerge. In this way, problems and hot issues can be solved more effectively and in a shorter period of time. The conversation method provides the structure for a group to think clearly together.

D. Preventing and Solving Problems and Conflict

Two girls were fighting on the playground one day. One of their classmates, trained in peer mediation, intervened.

Objective Level: "Mary, what happened here?" "She hit me." "Now Suzanne, you tell me what happened." "I hit her because she pulled my hair."

Reflective Level: "How did you feel when this happened?" "It made me really mad." "How do you think she felt?" "She was just as mad as me."

Interpretive Level: "Why do you think this fight happened?" "Because we both wanted the swing."

Decisional Level: "What could we do to solve this?" "I'll let her go for a while if she gives it to me next."

The use of the conversation method allows people to articulate their reactions, hear others' reactions, and use them as information as they build a larger understanding of the problem. This allows them to solve their problem. Participants do the work of creating their own solutions.

E. Evaluating and Taking Responsibility for Learning

A high school math teacher on interview night, facing an 18-year-old student who was not doing well and his mother, asked the student a few questions.

Objective Level: "Tom, here are the marks I have for you, the ones that are missing, and your current overall mark. What questions do you want to ask me about this data?

Reflective Level: What parts of this picture are you most satisfied with? What parts of this concern either of you?

Interpretive Level: Where do you discern gaps? What do you think are the underlying problems? How is this class important to you?

Decisional Level: What can you do about this? What help do you need from me or from your parents? Here are the times I'm available to help when you need it. What times would be best for you?"

Used in this way, the conversation method can facilitate a developing partnership between the student, teacher, and parent in the student's learning, with the student put into the position of taking responsibility for the decisions.

What Is in This Book

For those who want to understand where this method came from and why it works, chapters 2 and 3 explore the theory and the history behind the Focused Conversation Method in the context of learning and teaching. Chapters 4 and 5 focus on how to use and lead the sample conversations, and how to develop your own focused conversations.

Following these are five chapters, each with around thirty sample conversations. The topics selected offer practical examples of how teachers and others related to schools have used the Focused Conversation method to deal with their deep questions and struggles about learning and teaching. Each chapter has conversations that can be used with students, with staff, and with parents and community members. They are intended as templates to give you a starting point for preparing your own unique conversations. Chapter 10 also has creative examples of the use of the four levels of the process beyond a simple conversation.

Chapter 6. Making Learning Meaningful
The examples in this chapter provide ways to solve the problems of teaching clear thinking, facilitating the capacity to think abstractly and probe meaning, and providing a logical structure to present information. They also address the motivation of students to learn and the problem of applying and making use of what is.

Chapter 7. Making Communication Effective in Groups
Examples are provided of conversations for staff meetings, student group projects, and parent councils which foster timely and effective communication, build shared understanding and respect, and allow a group of people to come to wise decisions.

Chapter 8. Preventing and Solving Problems

These conversations demonstrate how students, teachers, administrators, and parents can use the conversation method to resolve misunderstandings and conflicts and resolve difficult problems, in one-on-one and group situations.

Chapter 9. Evaluating Learning

The examples in this chapter provide conversations for self-evaluation, as well as evaluating performance and accomplishments of both students and staff in an effective and fair manner that allows for growth.

Chapter 10. Creative Applications

In this chapter are some specific examples of creative applications of the four-level process. There are sets of conversations that work together to enhance learning, and other unique, creative applications of the four steps of the process.

In the Appendix, there is a list of sample questions for each level of the conversation method, for use with the worksheet forms to create your own conversations. The index includes myriad details from the conversations and examples used in the book to help you refer back to them easily. Finally, there are some blackline worksheets for creating conversations.

Additional conversations for the school as a workplace can be found in the book, *The Art of Focused Conversation: 100 Ways to Access Group Wisdom in the Workplace.*

CHAPTER 2

The Structure of the Focused Conversation Method

Of course, intellectual learning includes the amassing and retention of information. But information is an undigested burden unless it is understood....And understanding, comprehension, means that the various parts of the information acquired are grasped in their relations to one another, — a result that is attained only when acquisition is accompanied by constant reflection upon the meaning of what is studied.
John Dewey

A Natural Method of Processing Life Experience

The Focused Conversation method analyzed in this chapter is not a new invention. The four stages simply flow from a natural internal process of perception, response, judgement, and decision.

Imagine a toddler learning about the world. She sees a red burner on a stove. She touches it. The pain makes her jump back and howl. As she sticks her fingers in her mouth, she eyes the burner and thinks to herself, "That hurts!" She decides to explore something else. The next time she sees a red burner, she remembers the pain of the first experience, connects the knowledge that a red burner will hurt you, and decides not to touch it (or perhaps to touch it gingerly, to test her new knowledge).

Now imagine a ten-year old, doing a science experiment with levers. She observes that lifting is easier as she makes a lever longer. She remembers what happened before when she lengthened a different lever. She extrapolates the pattern that lifting always takes less work with a longer lever, and tests to see if her hypothesis holds true in another situation. Then she concludes what the rule is for levers and writes it down in her own words.

Imagine a high school student reading *Romeo and Juliet*. First he gains clarity on the words and what they mean, perhaps by reading them out loud. This triggers a set of associations with his own experiences of girls and parents, and movies he has seen. He interprets the actions of Romeo and Juliet through his own experience, then decides whether he likes the play or not. Or perhaps he changes his interpretation of his own experience based on what happens in the play, then acts differently toward his own girl-friend or parents.

Each of these learners:
• encounters the external world (objective level)
• associates internal experiences with it (reflective level)
• finds meaning (interpretive level),
• makes a conclusion or decision based on all of the above (decisional level)

These four levels describe the natural process of the human mind of which we are usually unconscious. The pattern of learning and processing can be described in basically the same way, whether it is done by an infant, a child, an adolescent, or an adult. The content changes, and as we gain experience, we have more internal associations to build on.

The Focused Conversation method works with these four stages of awareness and shifts the scope of activity from individual reflection on life to shared insight of a group. The conversation focuses on a particular topic. It uses questions to get at the concrete dimension of the situation, the emotive responses, interpretations of it, and the decision required.

Roots of the Method

Throughout the ages, we have tried to understand how we think. How people process ideas and experience is at the root of the four-level Focused Conversation method. Much of our present theory is developed from the work of people like Jean Paul Sartre, Edmund Husserl, and Søren Kierkegaard. They recognized that when a human being is thinking, reflecting or making a decision, complex processes are involved. As Edgar Schein points out in *Process Consultation*, our nervous system is a data-gathering system, an emotional processing system, a meaning-creation system and a decisional/implementing system, all at the same time. We observe what is going on around us. We react to it internally. We recruit our cognitive abilities to make sense of it, and we draw out the implications for action. At each level we forge links in this chain of awareness to process our lives.

How We Encounter Life

This method is based on some assumptions about how we encounter life and how we process information about it, drawn from observations of people in many cultures.

First, the method assumes that we find the reality of life in the palpable, observable, sensory world. We discover it in empirical experience. We start with what we see, smell, touch, taste, and hear.

Second, it assumes that authentic feelings, emotions, and associations arise from our empirical experience—whatever we encounter. This internal data is just as real as the externally observable data, and must be considered seriously in interpreting meaning and making decisions. It is important to note that this data from internal experience is just as empirical as that from outward perception, although we often pay it little attention. Daniel Goleman's book *Emotional Intelligence* reminds us that a large education job is needed to re-establish people's feelings and emotions as an integral part of being human. Noticing and recording our internal experience allows us to be conscious about it and prepares us to examine and use it.

The third presupposition is that we create meaning out of the mundane encounters in the midst of life, rather than find it in something detached from ourselves and our experience. Meaning is something we all have to work at constantly, through processing the actual life we have on our hands.

Fourth, the method assumes that processing insight about life involves projecting that insight out into the future. If we do not decide future implications for action, our reflection is stuck on viewing internal responses or theoretical implications, which never connect back to the world. Application of learning is the final stage of processing.

A Whole-System Process

Our four-stage thinking is a total process. It uses all the body's resources to come to terms with an object or experience: the senses, memories and feelings. It uses left and right brain, intuition and reason. It involves the volitional faculty to push the process through to decisions. In this sense, the focused conversation is a whole-system tool.

How the Stages Interact

The four relationships or stages just described are depicted in this diagram.

This image relies on a postmodern understanding that we encounter the world not as a series of isolated objects and substance, but as a bundle of relationships. The four vertical bars represent this bundle of relationships. This is one picture, not four. Imagine it is an animated video, building from left to right. Each level builds on data from the levels before it.

Some might wonder why such a natural thinking process needs a structure to guide a conversation through it. Laura Spencer comments in *Winning Through Participation*,

> In much of our education and training we are taught to short-cut this [thinking] process and move directly to...evaluate and judge things like a poem, a political system, a person's promotional potential, or the source of a problem, without first gathering all the objective data available. We are also taught that emotional responses are irrelevant and should be avoided or repressed. Once at the interpretive level, we often stop there, never formulating a response that leads to action.

Applying the Method to Structure Effective Conversations

Up to this point, we have talked about four levels of a thinking process that individuals go through. We can use this four-level process as a framework for creating questions to engage a group in dialogue. When a group processes the four levels together through a Focused Conversation, each individual's observations, experience, and insight enrich the whole group's learning in a structured way.

The focused conversation method uses questions at four levels:

• *The objective level:* questions about facts and external reality, or impressions
• *The reflective level:* questions to call forth immediate personal reaction to the data, an internal response, emotions or feelings, hidden images and associations with the facts. Whenever we encounter an external reality (data at the objective level) we experience an internal response.
• *The interpretive level:* questions to draw out meaning, values, significance, and implications.
• *The decisional level:* questions to elicit resolution, bring the conversation to a close, and enable individuals or the group to make a decision about the future.

These four levels of reflection form a template or pattern from which innumerable conversations can be drawn. If you compare the three learning vignettes from the beginning of this chapter with this process, you will notice that the flow of the levels of questions reflects the way people process information. I call it "how people think clearly, when they think clearly". It can be used to process any experience and deepen awareness.

Let's look at these four levels in more detail.

The Objective Level

The dictionary defines *objective* as external to the mind, dealing with outward things, or exhibiting facts uncolored by feelings or opinions. Objective includes things like data, facts and external reality or what someone called "D.O.D."—Directly Observable Data. Without work at the objective level, the group cannot be sure everyone is really talking about the same thing. Like the blind men touching the elephant, they may miss the whole picture, which is derived from putting their different perspectives together.

The first questions of the conversation get out the facts. They are usually sensory questions: What do you see? hear? touch? smell? taste? Depending on the topic, some senses, especially sight and sound, may be more relevant than others. A reflection on a multicultural festival will include questions about smells and tastes, just as a conversation on a sculpture will be sure to employ a question about touch, or the feel of the sculpture's surface. The right questions depend on what data is relevant. Sometimes there are questions of historical fact, for example, what did John actually say?

Because objective questions are easy to answer, the facilitator of an over-eager or over-sophisticated group may be tempted to downplay or omit them. But if five people experience the same thing, they have five different experiences. If the group is to think together, they need to have a shared foundation of all their experiences. The facilitator's courage to simply ask the questions firmly in spite of any initial resistance facilitates the realization that each person's unique perception of the data is important for the group to see the whole picture.

In a learning process, clarifying the concrete, observable data grounds the learner in reality.

In the example of the science experiment, hypothesizing how levers work without observing them would be simple guesswork, not real insight. A conversation between teachers about whether new education legislation is good or not without looking through its contents would probably go in circles, with various unconfirmed assumptions about the contents and its writers in play.

THE OBJECTIVE LEVEL IN A NUTSHELL

Focus of the questions	Data, the "facts" about the topic, external reality
What it does for the group	Ensures that everyone deals with the same body of data and all the aspects
Questions are in relation to	The senses: what is seen and heard and touched, etc.
Key questions	What objects do you see? What words or phrases stand out? What happened?
Traps and pitfalls	Asking closed questions, or questions not specific enough; no clear focus; Ignoring objective questions because "they are too trivial"
If this level is omitted	There will be no shared observation of what the group is discussing; the various comments may seem disrelated

The Reflective Level

Next comes the reflective stage in which the participants examine their personal responses to the topic. The questions for this level are concerned with feelings, moods, memories, and associations. By associations we mean trains of thought starting with "That reminds me of…" Both positive and negative reactions provide important information about a topic. This kind of internal data is just as real and important as objective data. If something worries me, it is important to get it said. Good interpretation and good decisions are be based on both external and internal data.

This level of the conversation acknowledges that we each have our own response to any situation, based on our previous experience. This level usually goes by very fast, and may not even be conscious. Catching immediate responses and acknowledging them allows them to be shared for personal and group use. To borrow a concept from Susan Langer in her book *Problems of Art*, the method "subjectifies the outward and objectifies the inward". It imbues what is outside the self with feeling and meaning. Inside, it can bring to the surface emotions and insights that we normally would not be aware of.

Here participants are asked questions which call on their more affective faculties. They are asked to actively reflect upon the information they acknowledged at the first level. Reflective questions include: What experiences do you associate with this? When have you been in similar situations? What surprised you? Where were you delighted? What upset you about this? Where did you struggle? Questions at the reflective level are not just simple requests for people to state their emotions. They draw out the specific objective data that triggered the reaction. The emotion, then, is grounded or related to something beyond itself. These questions illuminate what part of something people react to, and whether it angers, excites, intrigues, frightens, or delights them. The questions ask participants to articulate images and associations that are triggered by the information.

Without reflective questions, hidden images, associations, or moods do not get shared. If no reflective questions are asked, the essential world of intuition, memory, emotion and imagination is never evoked. Information is left at arm's length, and participants struggle with its relevance to their own lives. Without the opportunity to deal with this level, some participants may sense their feelings are deemed irrelevant. Later, they may air their reactions, but in the absence of any structural way to process them further, it is to no avail. Without objectifying the subjective in this way, people may be stuck, saying, "something happened", or "I feel bad", over and over. Articulating the reflective level allows participants to escape from repeating the loop between the external data and the internal response, and move on to interpreting the meaning of the situation. Evoking the personal connections at this stage is a powerful tool for learning and motivation. A group of educators who designed a peer mediation process for elementary school students noted that even when the questions about reactions are left out, children say their reactions and feelings anyway. When a students in a classroom can see that the characters in a story remind them of their own families, they are in a position to draw out the lessons of the story to their own lives. When students are encouraged to articulate both their reluctance to dissect a frog, and their wonder at the intricacy of a living being, their learnings from the experiment are enhanced a thousandfold.

THE REFLECTIVE LEVEL IN A NUTSHELL

Focus of the questions	Internal relationship to the data
What it does for the group	Reveals individuals' initial responses and validates their experience
Questions are in relation to	Associations, memories, feelings, moods, or emotional tones
Key questions	What does it remind you of? Which part surprised you? What delighted you? Where did you struggle?
Traps and pitfalls	Limiting the discussion to an either/or survey of likes and dislikes; Asking vague or broad questions that don't evoke relevant personal associations; Asking questions that demand embarrassingly personal answers
If this level is omitted	The world of intuition, memory, emotion, and imagination is ignored, and no shared personal experience is articulated on which to build meaning

The Interpretive Level

The third area of questioning is the interpretive level where the real grappling is done with the meaning of a topic. The interpretive responses build on objective data, and the associations or feelings from the reflective level. Interpretive questions highlight the layers of meaning and purpose that people ascribe to situations and responses. They invite a group to create the significance or importance of an occasion. A clue word at this level is "why". Interpretive questions help people build a "story" of what is happening. The question of values or ethics may appear, as in "What values does this reveal?"

This level is extremely important for learning, since there is an emphasis on meaningful connections, integration, understanding, and comprehension. Once the information is acknowledged and previous experience with it is made conscious, critical thinking, analysis and synthesis can happen. With questions such as "What is this story about?" or "How might the chemical reaction of soda and an acid apply to baking a cake?", students can make astounding connections with patterns that relate to their own life experience.

THE INTERPRETIVE LEVEL IN A NUTSHELL

Focus of the questions	The life meaning of the topic
What it does for the group	Draws out the significance from the data for the group; focuses on learnings
Questions are in relation to	Layers of meaning, purpose, significance, implications, "story", values, patterns. Considering alternatives, options. Comprehension
Key questions	Why is this happening? What is this all about? How does this compare? What does all this mean for us? How will this affect our work? What are we learning from this? What is the larger pattern emerging? What is the insight?
Traps and pitfalls	Inserting pre-cooked meaning that prevents real insight; over-intellectualizing or over-abstracting; judging responses as right or wrong
If this level is omitted	Group gets no chance to make sense out of the first two levels. No higher-order thinking goes into decision-making

For meetings, this is the level where people can see relevance, explore values, and sort out implications. Many conflicts can be bypassed, as the group explores the various facets of the topic's significance before decisions are made.

This level may well require the most time and the most focused questions, since the questions call for a deeper response. Several tightly focused questions will take learning to a higher level, such as these about the movie *Schindler's List*: What kind of a man was Schindler? What did he accomplish? From what you've seen in this movie, what do you think were his values? Where in the world today is harassment of specific ethnic or religious groups going on? What would it look like today to take an ethical stand?

The Decisional Level

The fourth part of the focused conversation is the decisional level where implications and new directions are discussed. Here, some kind of resolve brings the conversation to a close. The questions allow people to take the data from the previous levels, and use it to make choices.

Some decisional questions allow people to name their own relationships to their situation. Here the names and titles people give to events or things reflect their choices about them. Other questions may call for short or long-term decisions. These may involve a written decision or may be in the form of actions. In the classroom, class exercises or homework assignments may extend or apply the learnings of the lesson at this level.

Without some decision, the conversation is largely a waste of time. This is the place where application of knowledge to the everyday world is explored.

THE DECISIONAL LEVEL IN A NUTSHELL

Focus of the questions	Resolution, implications, application, new directions
What it does for the group	Makes the conversation relevant for the future
Questions are in relation to	Consensus, implementation, action, summarizing, application of knowledge, future directions
Key questions	How might you use this? How would you summarize your learning? What decision is called for? What are your next steps?
Traps and pitfalls	Forcing a decision when group is not ready or avoiding pushing group for decision
If this level is omitted	Learning is not consolidated, and the responses from the first three levels are not applied or tested in real life

You may have begun to get hints in this chapter that the Focused Conversation method was developed within a milieu of a good deal of research into education. If you are interested in that context of research, Chapter 3 explores it in detail. For practical procedures on how to design a specific Focused Conversation for your own use, go to Chapter 4.

The Research behind the Method

The art of remembering is the art of thinking;...when we wish to fix a new thing in either our own mind or a pupil's, our conscious effort should not be so much to impress and retain it as to connect it with something else already there. The connecting is the thinking; and if we attend clearly to the connection, the connected thing will certainly be likely to remain within recall.

William James

The Birth of the Conversation Method

The Institute of Cultural Affairs (ICA) began using the Focused Conversation method as a way for university students and adults to reflect on art forms in classes and weekend seminars around 1954. The professors found it helped their students to use a painting or a movie as a "slice of life" to test and apply their learnings from a course. The Focused Conversation method helped students to find deeper meaning and connect that learning with their everyday lives.

Brian Stanfield tells this story in *The Art of Focused Conversation*:

In a conversation on Picasso's painting *Guernica*, professor Joe Mathews asked his students to describe the objects in the painting. Then he invited them to look at their inner response. "OK", he said, "Now I want you to think about what sound you hear coming from the painting. I'm going to count to three, and then all of you make the sound you hear. Make it as loud or as quiet as you feel it should be. Ready? One, Two, Three!" The room exploded in howls of pain and rage. The door flew open and two students from the hallway stuck their heads in, their expressions resembling the faces in the painting itself. In stunned silence, they heard the teacher ask, "Where do you see this painting going on in your life?"

The results were startling. These students had thought of art as "a cultural thing", or "a decorative object". Now they saw their lives intimately involved with and reflected in art. They saw the art form as a force challenging their habitual stance towards life. Said one participant, "Suddenly I saw that these art forms were making a claim on me. They were saying, "Wake up! Live your real life."

Mathews' peers at the university joined his experimental approach to teaching. They tried various styles of participatory reflection in different courses. Eventually, they developed a format fluid enough to fit many subjects, yet structured enough to be described as a method. Voila! — the birth of the art form conversation.

The Focused Conversation method, or the art form method as the teachers called it, was further developed as a fundamental tool for allowing students to consciously develop their own images. The 19th century philosopher Søren Kierkegaard's exploration of consciousness sparked an idea of helping students work with the process of consciousness.

In *The Art of Focused Conversation*, Brian Stanfield says, "Kierkegaard and the phenomenologists described the self as a series of relationships or awarenesses that observed what was going on in life, reacted internally to those observations, created meaning or insight out of both of these, and drew out the implications or decisions implicit in that insight or meaning."

"The self is a relation [four vertical bars], *which, in relating itself to itself* [first arrow], *and willing itself to be itself* [second arrow], *grounds itself transparently in the power that posits it* [third arrow]".

Søren Kierkegaard
The Sickness Unto Death

If one takes Kierkegaard seriously, education is about expanding the consciousness of each student, so that choices and decisions become informed and self-aware. The conversation method is a tool that systematically and gently expands consciousness. At the objective level, students focus their awareness on what is objectively there before them. Then at the reflective level, students notice and articulate their inner images associated with the situation. At the interpretive level, they can self-consciously examine the relevance of these images. Finally, at the decisional level, they can choose how those images will affect their lives and actions.

The insight augmented the application of the theory of Imaginal Education, which was being developed by teachers on the staff of the Institute of Cultural Affairs.

The Theory of Imaginal Education

When ICA moved to the Fifth City community in Chicago's West Side, the staff founded a community preschool. The challenges of creating quality early childhood education in the inner city catalyzed a new research effort. The staff wanted effective ways of working with young children to provide a rich environment and a positive self-image that could make a lasting difference in their lives. Starting in 1965, public school teachers from across North America gathered in summer research assemblies with ICA staff and Fifth City Preschool staff to study, learn and reflect on their experience in teaching. They called their developing theory of knowledge and learning Imaginal Education.

The key research question was "How do people learn, and how does their behavior change as a result of their learning?" From this research came the theory of imaginal education, which has several basic tenets:

1) People operate out of images. That is, everybody has images of who they think they are, of how the world operates, and where they fit.

2) Images determine behavior.

3) Messages that reach a person affect the images he or she has, reinforcing them, adding new data, conflicting with them, or changing them entirely.

4) Images can change.

5) When images change, behavior changes.

The research into the role of images in education was based on work by Kenneth Boulding. In *The Image*, he explained how images underlie behavior, how they are created, and how they change or resist change. Marshall McLuhan, in *The Medium is the Message*, proposed that images created by different forms of media have as much effect as the content carried by the media. This theory suggested that messages are carried by the style or medium of teaching as well as the content that is taught. Paulo Friere's work, *Pedagogy of the Oppressed*, also had a profound influence. Friere demonstrated how the content of literacy training could have a powerful impact on the inner image of victimization students may carry, and lead them to a new capacity to change their situations.

Recent brain and learning research strengthens the theory of Imaginal Education. David Perkins, in his book *Smart Schools*, says,

> There is an important connection between a pedagogy of understanding and this notion of mental images. . . . . What do people have in their heads when they understand something?

> Contemporary cognitive science has a favorite answer: mental images (many psychologists would say "mental models" to mean the same thing). Roughly defined, a mental image is a holistic, highly integrated kind of knowledge. It is any unified, overarching mental representation that helps us work with a topic or subject....Mental images...concern very basic things such as the layout of your home or the shape of a story. But mental images can also concern very abstract and sophisticated matters.

Karen Olness, interviewed by Bill Moyers in *Healing and the Mind*, observes that when children use their imaginations, there is an impact on physiological responses. She says "my intuition is that whatever energy is associated with the construction of images and the process of thinking transmits a message to a cascade of body processes".

Many of the teachers who had begun the work on imaginal education continued to work together in an education guild. In a section called "Growing through Image Shifting" in one of their early papers they summarized their approach:

> Writers like McLuhan and Boulding have pushed us to realize that everyone has "images" that give form to one's world and determine behavior. Since new data inconsistent with operating images can challenge those images, it is clear that learning is a perpetual dynamic of re-imaging the "real". When Freud uncovered the unconscious processes of the psyche, he shattered every human being's image of itself as a simple rational being. Educators themselves know how their images affect their own behavior and that of their students. Experiments have shown that teachers who image a student as bright treat the student as indeed bright, regardless of the objective evidence of brightness. Furthermore, the student begins to image herself as bright, and to behave as if she were bright. Powerful images can release potential that seemed not to have been there. Images can also block potential and destroy motivation.
>
> Every image is formed out of messages of many kinds — from self, from family and friends, from the immediate environment, and the world at large. Most of these messages we handle easily; they conform to our present images of the way things are. But education happens when the messages contradict our present images in such a way that they are given up in favor of better images — images that illumine the messages. Learning is the process of re-imaging one's self and the world around it. This kind of imaginal learning is a [dramatic and sometimes] painful process involving the dying and rebirth of images, precious images which hold [our lives and] the world together.

Using Messages as a Teaching Tool

Imaginal Education, as described by the Institute staff in the *Fifth City Preschool Manual*, is "the process by which messages are intentionally directed to a person's images in order to give the opportunity for a change of image".

The imaginal approach recognizes that the messages we receive from the world interact with the values we hold. Those messages that are in alignment with our values get through to us and affect our underlying images. Those that are contrary to deeply held values may have little or no effect on our images. Some messages directly affect the values themselves. A teacher conscious of how her actions send messages to her students becomes aware that she is working with the values of her students. The manual described the role of messages like this:

> The imaginal educator creates messages which give a student an opportunity to change his image. However, change finally remains within the decisional realm of the student; the teacher cannot force an image change, but can only send messages. Because a

student's images are finally beyond the teacher's control, the teacher is released to build a model for what he sees as a desirable change in the student.

Messages can be consciously employed to influence positive images of students. Fifth City Preschool teachers began each day with a strong message about the potential of their young students:

Teacher:	*Students* (shouting in unison):
"Who are you?"	"I'm the greatest!"
"Where do you live?"	"In the universe!"
"Where are you going?"	"To bend history!"

Sending Messages with both Structure and Content

The research on changing images led to an understanding that content was only a part of the education received by the child. As Jerome Bruner says in *The Process of Education*, "the structure, not the content, of a discipline is the key to comprehension and retention".

The school is a whole system, which affects the lives of all the people involved in it, including students. The structure of a school sends many messages. When everyone must line up in straight lines when a bell rings, one message is that the student is subject to external rules and must subject their own needs to the group. When, on the other hand, children are allowed to run willy-nilly into the school at will, the message is that the individual's immediate wants are more important than group order. When active boys are continually reprimanded for not sitting still, the message is that one's internal physical needs and feelings are irrelevant and must be repressed in favor of order and quiet. Many of the things that children learn in school are messages that are conveyed by process and structure, and these are often as powerful as the content that the school intends to teach. Verbal messages may say one thing, and structures or environment may communicate another message. When the professed message is that education is about communication, yet children are not allowed to talk to one another, these messages contradict one another. When messages contradict each other, confusion or unclarity generate counter-productive behavior.

When we are unconscious of the messages our actions send, they may have unintended effects. A teacher I know told a mother after school one day in front of her six-year-old son, "He's lazy!" The message was very strong, and the boy's image of himself as a lazy person who couldn't learn became deeply embedded. After that, the boy consistently behaved out of that image in school. He rarely finished his work, and refused to try new things. At home, however, he worked hard at challenging tasks. In grade 9, another teacher gave the boy consistent messages that he was smart and a hard worker by praising his work and his efforts, and his school performance took a major turn upward.

Whether we intend to or not, we are communicating messages to our students that have an impact on their operating images. When we are conscious that our messages to students about themselves affect their operating images and therefore their behavior and actions, we cannot reduce our role to transferring information alone.

A consistent process and structure of thinking used throughout a school teaches all who are there, sometimes as much as the content of what is being talked about. The use of the conversation method can be as important in staff meetings, and on the phone with parents, as it is in the classroom. Students observe teachers and parents making decisions or working together, and copy the model. When that is consistent with the content that is being taught, the message is stronger, and has more impact on the images and thus the behavior of students.

The use of the Focused Conversation method, as a consistent process with students, structurally teaches students to think clearly about subjects. It gives the message that information is processed through reflecting on one's own experience, exploring its meaning, then acting upon it. The pattern of how to process information stays with a student long after the content is forgotten.

The *Fifth City Preschool Manual* lists ways to use the Focused Conversation method to help students develop a sense of responsibility:

- to have an ever broader base of objective data about the world and his particular situation upon which to base his decisions,
- to see more and more possible alternatives from which to choose,
- to project with skill and depth the implications of the possibilities for himself, others and the future,
- to decide, in the midst of ambiguity, that alternative which appears most responsible, or will best care for the most people.

The early development of imaginal education occurred in the real-life "lab" of a crowded inner city, where the luxury of teaching small groups was a pipe dream and the capacity to work together was a clear imperative. This mandated a focus on how to teach large groups of students effectively. The theories of cooperative learning developed by Johnson and Johnson, where students work together to create a product using the gifts and wisdom of each individual and thereby learning team skills, have a strong affinity to the methods of imaginal education. The structure of learning together gives the message to students that cooperative behavior in large groups is possible and preferred. The use of the conversation method encourages listening to all perspectives, and guides participants to deeper thinking and consensus, rather than encouraging the development of positions and arguing them. The conversation method also works well to help clarify assignments and to make group decisions.

Kenneth Boulding clearly states that authentic image-change is not forcing a person to change their images. We can send messages, but it is up to the person to change images. From this perspective, the teacher is a guide of learning, but cannot force a student to learn. The conversation method can be used to bring awareness to the messages that a student is deciding to accept. In this way, a student is encouraged to take responsibility for his or her own learning.

In such an approach to education, the job of the teacher may become easier and harder at the same time. In many ways, guiding the students to build their own knowledge through reflection relieves the teacher of the burden of knowing all the answers. However, it also removes the "cookbook" approach of teaching, where there is simply data to be downloaded from the text and the teacher into the student. Instead, the teacher becomes a catalyst to a three-part dialogue (or trialogue) process between the information, the student, and the teacher. When students and the teacher reflect together, everyone learns.

As OliveAnn Slotta says in *The Image-Based Instruction Workbook*,

> This ... approach offers a change from curriculum-driven to inquiry-driven classrooms, a change from the teacher role of "expert" to that of "guide". . . . We have noticed that when students see teachers excited about the connections that emerge among the various disciplines, they get excited, too. And surely no one among us would mind if the next decade in education became the decade of truly involved students.

Complementary Learning Theories

At the same time that the Focused Conversation method and the theory of imaginal education were being developed, other educators were looking at how the brain processes information and people learn. Several of them articulated similar processes, which have been compared with the conversation method.

At each step of the Focused Conversation method, different learning styles as identified by David Kolb in his *Learning Style Inventory* are evoked. At the objective level, "concrete experiential" learning is used. The reflective level brings out the "reflective observation" style. At the interpretive level, the "abstract conceptualization" style is honored. And at the decisional level, "active experimentation" is the favored mode. Using the conversation method allows all the students' preferred learning modes to contribute in turn to the group's learning. It also stretches each student beyond his or her preferred learning style. Bernice McCarthy says about her 4-Mat System, based on Kolb's learning styles, "The 4-Mat system moves through the learning cycle *in sequence*, teaching in all four modes and incorporating the four combinations of characteristics. The sequence is a natural learning progression."

Alma Flor Ada, creator of a bilingual reading program in California, uses a closely related four-step process as a basis for understanding reading texts. As she describes the process:

The Methodology of Creative Education ... views the learning process as centering on the learner, who is encouraged to develop critical thinking skills and an attitude of creative response in the face of real-life situations . . . .

In every act of real learning there are four phases:

Descriptive phase: In this initial phase the children receive information; that is, they learn what the text says ... Such questions are undoubtedly important, but they are not enough. A discussion that stays at this level suggests that reading is a passive, receptive, and in a sense, domesticating process.

Personal interpretive phase: Once the information has been presented, the children are invited to weigh it against their own experiences, feelings, and emotions. This step is extremely important. It fosters the reading process by bringing it within the children's grasp and thus making it more meaningful .... What is more, it helps the children understand that true learning occurs only when the information received is analyzed in the light of one's own experiences and emotions ....

Critical phase: Once the children have compared and contrasted what is presented in the reading with their personal experiences, they are ready to move on to a critical analysis, to the level of generalized reflection. The questions asked at this stage will help the children draw inferences about the information presented....

Creative phase: ...The process is completed only when the children can draw on [the awakening of critical awareness] in order to make decisions regarding the world around them....They will feel ...they are in a position to make decisions for improving and enriching their lives....It is a question of their beginning to assume responsibility for their own lives, for their relations with others, and for conduct within their sphere of action.

Creating Curriculum

Spiral curriculum

Another dimension of imaginal education is the related concept of a "spiral curriculum", which grew out of a theory proposed by Jerome Bruner. Bruner said that "Any subject can be taught to any child at any age in some form that is honest." In *The Process of Education*, he elaborated:

A spiral curriculum (is) the idea that in teaching a subject you begin with an "intuitive" account that is well within the reach of a student, and then circle back later to a more formal or highly structured account, until, with however many more recyclings are necessary, the learner has mastered the topic or subject in its full generative power. Another way of saying the same thing might be to say "Readiness is not only born but made." The general proposition rests on the still deeper truth that any domain of knowledge can be constructed at varying levels of abstractness or complexity. That is to say, domains of knowledge are made, not found: they can be constructed simply or complexly, abstractly or concretely.

The application of this concept, taking what a student understands and extending thought and curiosity from that point, creates the possibility of "comprehensive curriculum". This suggests that one can teach important content about the world to a student at any level of development with appropriate tools and curriculum. For example, the complex concept of air pressure in fluid dynamics can be introduced to a four-year-old by observing what happens when a glass is submerged in dishwater, turned upside down, and lifted to the surface of the water. A focused conversation on the experience allows the student to explore the possible causes of the effect, and design further experiments to discover more about the phenomena. A discussion about a fight between schoolyard gangs or cliques may allow insight about the causes of war in human history.

The process of teaching content is always in tension with facilitating learning. Since no one is a blank page, but a collection of previous experiences to build on, the teacher does not have to teach what students already know, but can provide extensions of knowledge. The teacher is relieved of the burden of always having to be an expert, and can learn along with the students. Each student has wisdom and can contribute to the group. As David Perkins notes in *Smart Schools*, education becomes 1) extending the *capacity* of students to think clearly, to apply learnings, and to work together, and 2) extending the *consciousness* of students so that they perceive more and make wise decisions (Emphasis in original).

The conversation method is a powerful tool to extend both the capacity and the consciousness of the student. The gap between theory and practice is bridged with questions at the decisional level, which lead to application. Often this is a neglected part of education. We have all heard of people who did well in solving arithmetic problems on exams, but could not use problem-solving processes in real life; or people who have degrees in psychology but can't apply it to everyday relationships. We can only verify if a student has really learned something if his behavior changes — that is, if he applies what he has learned in real life.

Tools to carry messages

As the research into how people's behavior is affected by images began to gel, teachers experimented with imaginal education in schools and preschools. They created curriculum and activities that would create positive images in order to affect their students' capacity to learn, grow, and take responsibility. Since different children respond best to different kinds of messages, diverse tools were developed to effectively reach a wide variety of students. A "tools chart" was developed, or a palette of activities and materials to teach various subjects, using different media, appealing to all the senses, and meeting a wide range of learning styles. The nine categories of tools included three literary media —drama, poetry, and prose; three rhythmic media — instruments, dance, and song; and three plastic media — architecture, sculpture, and visual art.

This development of comprehensive learning tools has been enriched by Howard Gardner's theory of multiple intelligences in his book, *Frames of Mind*. Gardner says, in essence, that there are multiple forms of intelligence. Everyone has intelligence, some forms of which are weaker and some stronger. We have traditionally measured only verbal-linguistic and mathematical-logical intelligence. However, there are at least six more: visual-spatial intelligence, kinesthetic or bodily intelligence, musical intelligence, intra- and inter-personal intelligences, and finally "natural" intelligence (knowing through nature). We learn content more easily through our stronger intelligences, and we can also strengthen our weaker ones. As any group of students has strengths in different combinations of intelligences, these can be used like an artist's palette to teach content in a way that reaches all the students in ways that they can easily learn. For example, teaching the alphabet by tracing the letters (kinesthetic and visual intelligence), telling a story based on each letter (verbal-linguistic intelligence), and singing the alphabet song (musical intelligence) will go a long way to ensure that everyone in the class learns the letters as easily as possible.

The conversation method can be used in conjunction with a variety of tools and intelligences. Using the conversation method to debrief classroom events deepens the learning experience. Since the method was originally developed to understand art forms, it is ideal for reflecting on visual creations. A highly effective use I have seen is to reflect on trust-building exercises done in a high ropes course with sixth and seventh grade students. In a very different way, the evaluation conversation with preschoolers in Chapter 9 asks questions at each level that require kinesthetic or visual responses as well as verbal ones. David Lazear, in *Teaching through Multiple Intelligences*, shares many examples of the use of the conversation method with curriculum events using different intelligences.

The conversation method takes the experiences that students have in the classroom, or in other situations, and extends their experience to deeper interpretation and application to life. When I was working with a preschool in the village of Bayad, in rural Egypt in 1977, the students in the preschool had an image of the world around them that was limited to immediate experience of their village. I had only a vague image of ancient Egypt, and that image had no connection with the present day. The preschool staff and I took the students on a field trip one day, walking our charges down to the river and crossing on a felucca, or sailboat, to the government building on the other side of the Nile in the provincial capital of Beni Suef. In the lobby of the government building was a large mural. As we stood in front of it, we used the conversation method to understand what was there. First we noted the step pyramid of Maidum on the far right, then farmers with hand tools and buffalo-drawn plows to the left of that, then a tractor, then a factory and city images on the left. As we recognized the right-to-left progression of the images and interpreted their meaning, thousands of years of history rolled out in front of us. The last question was "What are we going to create in the future here?" As the teachers, the children, and I left to go back to the village, our images of who we were and where we fit in history had taken on a new dimension. We had a much larger sense of our responsibility to build on the wisdom of the past and create a human future for rural Egypt.

Planning curriculum events

With thoughtful planning of lessons, the concepts and tools of imaginal education can be applied in highly motivating curriculum events. In a lecture for an Imaginal Education course in 1981 on the topic of "comprehensive design", Kaye Hayes outlined the use of the four levels of the Focused Conversation process in lesson planning. She suggested four levels for a lesson plan format: 1) impingement, or initial impact (such as a dramatization of some sort); 2) awareness, or the beginning of rational understanding of content (such as a lecture or visual that communicates content); 3) involvement, an exercise or way for the students to participate; and 4) responsibility, getting the student to ask questions or begin to apply the content.

In 1986 the "kaleidoscope teaching strategy" was developed at the Atlanta Teachers' Institute led by Keith Packard, OliveAnn Slotta, and others. Ronnie Seagren summarizes the goals of this teaching strategy in *Approaches that Work in Rural Development, Volume 3:*

> The spiral journey of learning is carried on in several ways:
> * *Expanding the context* beyond the self as the primary frame of reference. A perceived connection to the broadest possible perspective of time, space and relationships enables the learner to operate out of hope for the future rather than fear.
> * *Stimulating the imagination* by encouraging the learner to view a situation from a variety of opinions and perspectives, and to 'see' reality not yet created.
> * *Beckoning participation* by creating opportunities for active involvement. When ideas are connected with people's real life questions, meaning and motivation are awakened.
> * *Encouraging critical thinking* by guiding the learner to relate information to inner resolve, will, and values. Ethical reasoning empowers an individual to operate responsibly and independently.
> * *Touching a person's depths* in order to build self-esteem and release human potential.

A lesson that stimulates imagination, beckons participation, expands the student's context, encourages critical thinking, and builds self-esteem is one that produces highly motivated students. Teachers can incorporate these five elements into their lesson plans using the Focused Conversation method as an integral tool.

For example, one year I taught four sessions on Australia to a Canadian second grade class. One lesson was intended to give students information on the settling of

Australia by Europeans. I had them imagine they were people living in "olden days", who were so poor that they had to steal bread to feed their children, were arrested and thrown into jail. They were put on a ship to the prison colony of Australia, leaving their families behind. Then I had all the children lie down on the carpet, tightly packed together, imagining that they were packed into the convict ship for several months, seasick from the waves, with only runny oatmeal to eat and no way to move. When they arrived in Australia, they had to find food to eat and build shelter in an unknown land, with red soil, strange grey-green vegetation, and people who looked like no people they had ever seen before. I then led a focused conversation on the experience, drawing out their feelings and their imagination. We explored what impact that would have had on them. Not only did they have a physical sense of the beginnings of white Australian settlement, but also they had very interesting thoughts on crime and punishment. The boys of the class, who were usually disruptively noisy, were attentive and creative in their participation.

Imagine what society would be like if students finished school with the capacity to observe events around them, to connect new information with their previous experiences, to interpret the impact and meaning of their experiences, and to act on their insights. As psychologist Jean Houston put it in a New York lecture in 1987, "We're living in the attic of ourselves. We don't use the first three floors, and the basement is locked, until it wells up in an explosion". Imaginal teaching gives tools to unlock the basement and relate inner and outer space. The possibility of using a much larger part of our consciousness in an effective manner is an awesome vision.

Part II
Application

CHAPTER 4

Preparing a Conversation

Curriculum must be connected with and relevant to the lives of students. Without this connection, students see no value in their learning and are not motivated to continue learning. Curriculum becomes useful only when it is relevant and meaningful to the students.

R. Bruce Williams

Is the Focused Conversation method the tool you really need for your situation? It may not be. You can't teach everything, or manage every meeting, with open-ended questions. A focused conversation will not tell students what they should know, or convince people to buy into your ideas. One way to test whether you should use a conversation is to look at the outcomes you want. If your objective is for the group to probe the implications of a topic and come to their own conclusions, a Focused Conversation method is an ideal tool.

If it is really necessary to simply transfer facts to students or staff members, you may need a lecture, a demonstration, or a memo. There are a few examples in Chapter 10 of presentations that are constructed using the four-level format as a structure. Keep in mind, however, that a conversation is often helpful for people to process the facts after they have been transferred. If you want people to process the information you have presented in depth, or to reach their own conclusions, a conversation will be useful following your presentation as part of a larger agenda.

Once you have considered a range of tools and decided that a focused conversation is appropriate, you can start preparing.

Preparatory Steps

A quality conversation begins with quality preparation. It is really worth the time to prepare. Advance preparation actually saves time, and it certainly gets better results. This chapter walks through the steps of preparing a quality conversation.

The conversations later in this book are already written out, ready for use. You can use many of them as they are. But the situations they are designed for are not often identical to your situation, and you will likely want to adapt them to your class or group and task.

To adapt a conversation, use the following steps as if you are creating a conversation from the beginning. The first step is to clarify your own focus and objectives. When you are ready to generate the questions, you can start your brainstorm of questions with the questions in the book, and add your own.

If there is no example similar to the conversation you need, you can use these same steps to prepare your own conversation from scratch.

There is a blackline worksheet in the appendix that will guide you through these steps to prepare your conversation. It's a good idea to use a pencil and sticky notes, so that you can refine your ideas as you go along.

1. Focusing the Topic

Determining the topic of a conversation usually seems like the easiest step, but it is not always so easy. Usually the topic is assigned or in response to a problem, but it is still important to pick a target topic and find a concrete place to begin. The conversation method works best on tightly focused topics, and it needs a concrete object or shared experience as a beginning point. It takes thinking time, and sometimes several experiments, to get this degree of clarity. Without focus, the group will talk in generalities, and will not know what is happening. Starting at an abstract or general level will obscure meaningful dialogue. A focused topic allows the group to articulate the objective data more clearly and probe more deeply at the interpretive level.

For example, the curriculum in social studies for the day calls for a discussion on the topic of politics. This is a broad, abstract concept at this level, and could imply many different focused conversations. Perhaps a focus might be on the experience of participating in a political rally by students in the room, or on recent political events in the news, or a textbook chapter on the development of political parties.

In another example, a parent group is meeting to consider student safety. More tightly focused topics might be "playground safety", or "bus safety", or "safety while crossing the street", or "how to deal with bullies".

Sometimes it is useful to try to write the intent of the conversation, and then come back to the topic. More than one rational aim, or an abstract one, is a hint that the topic is too large.

2. Write Down the Intent of the Conversation

Every time we lead a conversation, we influence the outcome through both the content and the process of the discussion. The content outcome or aim is the knowledge and understanding that the individuals and the group take away at the end. The internal change in the participants and the group is the process outcome. When we articulate the goals in advance, we can design a conversation to accomplish them.

The *rational aim* is the practical goal or the concrete learning of the conversation. This is the content outcome. The rational aim of a conversation in a lesson plan might be to understand a math process, or to discover the insights in a Shakespeare play, or to consolidate learning from the past week's work. For a staff meeting it might be a decision about how to solve a problem, or understanding the implications of a new school board policy

The *experiential aim* refers to the inner image or change in the group that the message that the process sends will affect. This is the process outcome. For example, the experiential aim of a lesson plan might be to increase students' confidence that they can learn a difficult concept, or to develop commitment to apply learnings, or to increase respect for each other. For a staff meeting it might be to strengthen commitment to carry out plans, or to have increased trust in the school team.

The first step in planning a conversation is to mull over these goals and write them down on your worksheet. Watch for your personal "right answers" and assumptions. If you discover at this point that you want the group to buy into your answer at the end, stop here and prepare a presentation instead.

Be prepared to revise and sharpen your aims as you work through your preparation, as the act of designing a conversation helps you to think through what is needed.

3. Ensure a Concrete Beginning Point for Your Objective Questions.

The conversation method starts with objective questions about a concrete object or shared experience that has observable data. Without a concrete beginning point, it is very difficult to ask objective questions. Starting with abstraction ensures that the conversation remains confusing. Most topics have several possible concrete beginning points.

Often we begin by getting the group to "define the terms". Starting a conversation in this way skips the objective and reflective levels and begins at the interpretive. The group is more able to define terms following a discussion that begins with something concrete and moves naturally through experience to meaning. For example, if you want a conversation to help develop an understanding of racism, it will work better to start with a very concrete beginning point such as a news article on a recent event, or a short story, or a skit acted out by students. Or even, as one teacher did, a Renaissance painting that portrays two men in Jewish clothing at a far corner of the painting, with their backs turned to the action of the painting. This gets people thinking about a real-life experience, object, or art form. If the opening question were, What do we know about racism?, you might start a lively argument, but it wouldn't be focused and might not be productive. When the conversation is built on a concrete shared experience, a very different discussion emerges which is more likely to be honest and lead to thoughtful responses.

In the same manner, a conversation on "safety on the playground" might start by displaying an overhead with playground safety statistics, or a video on playground safety, or by focusing on a recent accident. Beginning with concrete reality allows powerful interpretations as people connect the starting point with their own reality.

4. Brainstorm Questions to Realize the Rational and Experiential Aims

Give your mind free rein to write down all the possible questions you could ask on the topic. Don't worry at this point about the order of the steps. Just review the topic, the rational objective and the experiential aim; then start brainstorming. Write questions down in any order, just as they occur to you, on paper or sticky notes. Let your creativity

---

Adapting the Questions for Different Ages, Maturity or Grade Levels:

When questions are asked in the order of the Focused Conversation method, children are guided to surprisingly deep levels of thinking. However, questions do change for different age levels. Several more specific objective level questions (Who were the characters in this story? What happened first?...then?.. then?..) work better for young children than one larger question (What was the plot of this story?), which can work better for more mature students. Older students may act as if objective questions are so obvious they don't need to answer them, but those who are confused will never admit it, and answers to the objective questions will ensure that everyone is working with all of the available information. Do not assume that it is necessary to skip one of the four levels for any age group.

Younger students may struggle more with the interpretive level, as they may not yet have a strong capacity for abstract thinking, but creative interpretive questions (What might happen next in this story?, or What might this be used for?) will extend the capacity they have. With very young children, some examples of possible answers will be useful (Did this happen because ... or because ...? rather than Why did this happen?), but they will only elicit honest participation if a wide range of possible answers is suggested rather than just having yes or no answers. More mature students will need more interpretive questions to explore meaning in more depth. Asking all four levels of questions will also include students at different levels of thinking, thus affirming each student.

---

flow. If you start crossing out questions you don't like, or arranging them in levels prematurely, you will interrupt the free flow of ideas. Just let the questions come. Using the sample conversations in this book or the question lists in the appendix may spark your creativity.

5. Select and Order the Questions You Will Ask

You won't need all the questions you wrote down, nor will they all be equally useful. Use your own best judgement to select the questions you will actually use. Review your rational and experiential aims, choose first the key questions that will accomplish your goals, then choose others that will work with the key questions.

Copy your chosen questions or plot your sticky notes into the columns on the worksheet. Within each level, rearrange the order of questions until each one flows easily into the next question. If you have used sticky notes, move them around to get the best sequence.

How Many Questions at Each Level?

Sometimes people ask: "How do I know how many questions to ask at each level?" Situations and needs differ. However, in general, each step needs to explore enough to generate sufficient information to proceed to the next level. To be specific: you need at least four questions, one at each level.

The objective level needs enough questions to produce a good sampling of data from which to draw conclusions.

Even a very short conversation usually needs two or more reflective questions that ask for very different reactions to give people permission to get out their real responses. Many people will not feel safe in articulating reactions different from others in the group unless you specifically ask for them.

Interpretive answers may need several additional questions to push for concrete, specific examples or to draw out a deeper level of thinking to support an opinion. Sometimes you need to explore each option with a series of questions using the first three levels, producing conversations within conversations. This demands special skill.

Two or three decisional questions can be helpful, depending on the conversation: one to objectify what has been decided, the second on "next steps", and sometimes a third on who will do what.

The conversations in the book give some models for particular kinds of situations.

---

6. Rehearse the Conversation in Your Head

Go over the conversation, asking yourself each question. Experience how the question strikes you, and ask yourself how your group would answer it. This gives you a participant's eye view of the questions. Look for transition and flow. You may find yourself saying, "I want to change that question. That is not what I really meant to ask." By doing the conversation with yourself first, you find out where the weak spots are, and you can handle them before the conversation begins. Some questions may need to be rephrased more simply. You may need to add more questions at certain points. Some questions may sound too formal. Others may work better in a different order. With each change imagine how you would feel as a participant.

The conversation process is really a flow, not just a set of steps. Working on the flow of the questions, one into the other, helps the group experience one seamless conversation in which answers flow as a stream of consciousness.

7. Prepare Your Opening Carefully

Opening comments serve some or all of these functions:

Invitation: You invite the group to participate in the conversation. "Let's explore what this means for all of you."

Focus: Name the focus of the conversation: "We're going to talk about the chemistry experiment you have just seen." You may need to share the rational aim of the conversation with the group so that they know where the conversation is going. Put the rational aim in words that make sense to your participants: "By the end of this conversation, you will understand the concept and know how to apply it to other problems." The opening establishes reference points to use later. Stating the topic and the main question allow the facilitator to keep the group on track with gentle reminders. Some groups prefer to know the process up front, and you might put the questions on a flipchart so that everyone can see them and hold their answers until the question is asked. Other groups don't need to know what process you will be using.

Context: Some words of context might say how the conversation relates to the group's concerns about the task, and why it is needed right now: "We need to discuss it now while it is still clear in our minds." Sometimes sharing the intended duration of the conversation puts a group at ease. "This conversation will take us about 20 minutes, and then we will have time for the next agenda item."

Forestall any objections. Deal up front with reasons for avoiding the conversation: "A quick conversation now will make it much easier for you to know what to put into your notebooks about the experiment."

Focus on the concrete beginning point. Focus participants' attention on the beginning point you have chosen. Pass out the paper, or call their attention to the experience they are recalling. "Let's start by looking at the handout."

Set ground rules. Clearly stating expectations of behavior during the conversation will make people more willing to participate. The group may need to be reassured that this is a safe environment to participate in. "In this conversation, we want to make sure everyone's views are heard; so if you don't agree with what other people are saying, you will also be encouraged to put your ideas on the table. There are no wrong answers." This is particularly important for students, since they may have experienced harsh judgment from teachers and other students for their ideas in the past, and may be afraid to participate.

Several of these functions can be combined in an opening statement or two.

Sometimes conversation leaders are tempted to "wing it" on the opening because they feel the questions are the heart of the matter. But careful thought on each sentence of the opening gives the leader a big advantage in getting the group on side and willing to discuss the topic at hand.

8. Prepare the Closing Carefully

In the same way, write down the words you will use to bring the conversation to a close. This saves you stumbling around at the end looking for a graceful way to get off stage. The conversation may have solved certain problems, but other problems remain. Don't try to pretend these don't exist. Say something like, "I guess we all noticed that this conversation did not really deal with the concerns raised by Jonathan and Amy. These are important matters, and I have noted them for the next class."

Don't forget to affirm the group's insights. If appropriate, say how the results of the conversation will be made available, or how you expect the group will use the results.

9. Reflect on the Conversation, the Group, and Yourself

After you have prepared the entire conversation, read it through as a whole, seeing how it flows. Make sure questions lead naturally from one to the next, without any sudden leaps. You may want to revise the wording of a couple of questions, or add or subtract questions. Prepare the timeline to allot how much time to spend on each level, and how long the conversation will take.

Now take a little time to reflect on the group and what's been happening to it lately, Ask yourself what kind of style will enable them to deal with the issue. Evaluate yourself, your biases, your strengths and weaknesses as a conversation leader.

10. Learning from Your Experience

After you have led the conversation, think about how the conversation actually happened. Note any changes you would make, because these will help you learn more about preparing and leading future conversations.

CHAPTER 5

Leading a Focused Conversation

There are ample opportunities to orient instruction toward higher levels of understanding, introduce and exercise languages of thinking, cultivate intellectual passions, seek out integrative mental images, foster learning to learn, and teach for transfer. The smart school makes the most of these opportunities.

David Perkins

You may be asking, "Why do we lead focused conversations? Aren't conversations meant to be spontaneous? Doesn't the attempt to lead a conversation destroy spontaneity and take the fun out of it?"

Although the Focused Conversation method is based on a natural pattern of thinking, we don't always think systematically. It takes discipline to learn to be aware of our thinking, and even more discipline to use that consciousness to continually think with clarity. With preparation and attentive listening, a facilitator can bring focus and increased creativity to a group's thinking. Even with a well-designed process, conversations may be rocky. Some people tend to speak a lot or forcefully and dominate the conversation. Others find it painful to speak out loud, and are rarely heard from. Participants often take the conversation in a direction that was not intended, or drop a provocative comment in where it was least expected. Conversation leaders can help a group avoid trivia, argumentation, or abstraction. When these common pitfalls are avoided, the conversation goes better. Individuals participate more freely, and data builds on data in an orderly fashion. The task of the conversation leader is to release the dammed-up genius, creativity, wisdom, and experience of the group and guide it towards a well-considered conclusion. This chapter will provide the reader with a basic level of preparation to lead a focused conversation.

How to Lead a Focused Conversation

Facilitator's Responsibility

The facilitator of a focused conversation takes responsibility for guiding the group to its own best thinking on a topic. The facilitator also takes responsibility for the messages of the process that affect the experience of the participants. This means careful preparation of the aims and the questions, but it also means listening carefully as the group responds. Questions may need to be added, skipped, or re-phrased to enable adequate reflection. Watching body language and tone of voice may also give clues to how the conversation is affecting the participants, and suggest the need for adjustment.

Facilitating a conversation takes much the same form whether it is with students, staff, parents, or community members. The conversation leader uses a number of techniques to make the group feel comfortable with participation and to keep them focused on the task.

1. Set a Suitable Environment

The space needs to be set for people to see and hear each other for a conversation to facilitate participation. A classroom set up in theatre style, where all eyes are on the person at the front of the room, sends a strong message that the only person who matters is the teacher. Move to the side or sit on a desk near a corner. When it is possible, move chairs, desks, or tables into a semi-circle or rectangle, so people have the opportunity to make eye contact with each other and see the front of the room as well. Make sure everyone can hear each other, and avoid distractions. Everything in the space needs to say, "Each participant is important, and the subject is important." When the setting communicates the message that people's ideas are respected, they will participate more respectfully in return.

2. Invitation

Invite the group to take their places. Let them get settled.

3. Opening

Start with some planned opening remarks. Give your opening statement about the purpose of the conversation, the topic, the history and importance of the topic, how the results will be used, or other necessary contextual information. Giving the group the questions at the beginning often allows them to hold their responses until the appropriate question is raised. For example, "Let's have a conversation about this topic and explore what we can come up with. Say what you think in answer to these questions. Your opinion is not being evaluated." Often it is helpful to establish some ground rules, such as "we will listen to each person's response to hear its wisdom".

4. The First Questions

If there are a manageable number of people participating, it helps to ask each participant to answer the first question. This acts as an icebreaker for everyone in the room. Make it a simple objective question that no one will have great difficulty answering. If the first question is: "As you read this story, what words or phrases caught your attention?" Say something like this: "For the first question, let's start with Ralph, and then go all the way round the table. Ralph, what is a word or phrase in the story that caught your attention?" After Ralph answers, look at the next person and wait for their answer. If there are more than 15 participants, it may be helpful to switch to another objective question about halfway through. Answers should flow smoothly, one after the other, and should be short. Dissuade anyone from trying to grandstand or make a speech. Tell them that the discussion of responses and recommendations will come later. If you suspect that some are quiet because they are afraid they might make a mistake, you can say, "There are no wrong answers in this conversation." Be sure that your behavior supports this statement. There may not be an immediate impact, but the continued use of the method throughout the year with respect for individual answers will create a culture of investigation and respectful sharing, where most students feel safe to participate.

Answering the objective questions can be both the easiest and the most difficult part of the conversation. Some people consider it childish to share obvious observations. They will want to leap immediately to give their opinion on the subject, their quick judgements on what should be done about it, or mention ideas that are triggered by the subject. You may have to help the group deal with objective questions. If they jump directly to an abstract reflection, you can repeat the question or clarify it, or you may ask something like "What did you read in the story that triggered that response?" Sometimes you might give an example such as, "I noticed the part where they shine their shoes for the fat lady."

You may need to remind participants to speak loudly enough that everyone in the room can hear, not just the conversation leader.

5. Subsequent Questions

Address subsequent questions to the whole group. On the second question, indicate that anyone can answer by saying, "Now, anybody …" This says you are not going to go round the table again, and anyone can answer in any order.

6. Getting off the Topic: What Do You Do?

Generally, if students or meeting participants get off the topic, it is not a discipline problem. The human mind is very associative, which makes straying away from the topic quite easy. However, since you are leading a focused conversation, focus is important. When you sense someone is veering away from the topic, affirm what they are saying as insightful or an important concern. Then recapitulate briefly what the group has said so far in response to the question. You may want to repeat the question, or the digression may signal it is time to move on to the next question.

7. What about Wrong Answers?

At times, a participant's answer will be factually, historically or geographically wrong. The teacher cannot let it pass, but how he responds will depend on the situation. In a classroom, the teacher may respond with "Can you point to where the book says that?" as a gentle correction that keeps the information straight without squelching a student. Other useful questions may be, "Why do you say that?", or "That doesn't match the understanding I've heard, please clarify it for me." Or the conversation leader may ask the group if there are other answers.

Sometimes people make offensive comments. The answer may be racist, sexist, or bigoted. It may be quite cynical. It is important to listen to the tone in which the comment was made. Some of these responses are unconscious, and the effect is unintended. Others are intended to get the group to react strongly, or to derail the conversation. It may also be the response of someone who wants to get their agenda on the table. It is important to honor the person but not to allow the person's comment to take over the conversation. If the facilitator thinks the group can absorb the comment, she can ignore it and move on. If he sees the group is visibly offended by it and looking to him to do something, the conversation leader can ask, "Would you say that in another way, please?" It may be necessary to stop the conversation to re-establish the ground rules.

Sometimes students give deliberately weird or "wrong" answers to test the teacher or the group. Many times merely accepting the answer and going on with no fanfare to the next student or the next question will discourage this behavior. It is often useful to ask the student "Why do you say that?" or "What triggered that line of thinking?" There may be creative thinking behind a strange answer. If the student is deliberately trying to be disruptive, he is respected as a person by probing his meaning, and challenged to think honestly. Sometimes asking the group to respond thoughtfully will help. A quick look at your experiential aim will keep you on track. If you want to encourage self-esteem, you will handle the provocation in such a way that will increase self-respect in all participants. For example, "That's very interesting." or "That's very creative." or "That's an important point of view." As students realize that you will accept their answers, they will allow themselves to put forward creative thinking.

If one participant's views seem strange to others, there is probably a good reason for them in that person's life experience. After all, we continue to grow by our effort to understand different viewpoints and insights, and this often involves letting go of our own preconceptions about life. At the same time, no piece is the whole picture. Everyone has a piece of the puzzle, but the whole picture comes together through hearing and understanding all the perspectives. When all the perspectives are heard, a more holistic picture appears, like a diamond with many facets. The object of the conversation is to draw out that many-faceted wisdom.

One of the most difficult challenges for teachers is to make sure that her agenda does not get on stage while he or she is facilitating a conversation. When the facilitator loses objectivity, the group knows it is being manipulated, and honest participation is lost, replaced with a reaction to the facilitator's agenda. Any teaching points that must be transmitted to the students from the teacher need to be separated from the conversation. This can be done as a presentation before or after the conversation. In the midst of a conversation, the teacher can change hats to become an expert, but the lines have to be clearly drawn: "Let me step out of my role as conversation leader and give you some important information to address your confusion."

8. Long or Abstract Answers: What Do You Do?

If the conversation leader asks vague or abstract questions, he will tend to get vague or abstract answers. Specific questions have a better chance of getting specific answers, and answers that have more useful meaning. "What is the story about?" is a vague question. Notice the difference in the kinds of answer you might get asking something specific like, "What insight does the main character have about her own life?" If you are getting abstract answers, try rephrasing the question.

If someone launches into a long or abstract answer, ask for a specific example: "Ben, I wonder if you could say that in fewer words," or, "Could you give us a particular example of that?" or "What is the key point you are making?" Such questions help the speaker clarify and ground their insights. Assure the speaker that your concern is that his point be understood. If vague statements go unclarified, the conversation cannot draw out deeper insight.

9. If an Argument Starts, What Do You Do?

Sometimes we assume that the only way to explore meaning as a class or a group is to debate pros and cons. In the conversation method, there is plenty of room for people to disagree with each other, but the emphasis is on clarifying and explaining responses, not attacking or defending them. This creates an atmosphere of thoughtfulness, rather than contradiction or argument. When people make bold declarations, ask for their supporting thought. Ask, "What led you to that conclusion?" If an argument starts between different participants, remind the group that all perspectives need to be honored, that everyone has wisdom, and everyone has a piece of the puzzle. Then ask if there are other viewpoints. For example, "What are other very different or opposing perspectives on this?"

In many groups and classes there are two or three people who need to comment or disagree with everything. When someone interrupts another, ask them to wait until the first person is finished. Then ask, "Now, what is your idea?" If one of these people tries to discredit others' replies, you might ask, "I see you do not agree with Jim's answer. So tell us how you would answer the question." Take care that your voice conveys interest rather than irritation. Let them answer the question as well, and let the contrasting views stand side by side as equal answers to the question. Then move the conversation on by allowing others to give other answers or by asking the next question. This allows the dis-agreement to add to the group's thinking, rather than to shut it down.

10. Closing

Bring the discussion to a close with a few words to sum up the group's conclusions, and to thank the participants. If you have made notes during the conversation, let the group know how the notes will be used. If appropriate, you might assure them you will make copies available.

Facilitating a Conversation Is Not Teaching Content

You may be asking, "Shouldn't students be guided toward the teacher's point of view? After all, isn't the teacher paid to be an expert?"

One important role of a teacher is to impart wisdom, experience, and tried-and-true knowledge to students. However, research shows that new information isn't retained unless a student relates new information to his previous information and images about the world. When we lead a focused conversation on a topic, we are genuinely asking students to do their own processing of the information, so that they can internalize its significance, come to their own decisions about it, and apply their learning to their own lives. An often-overlooked role of a teacher is to evoke students' thoughtful response and integra-tion of knowledge. The open-ended questions in a conversation allow students to process information in a way that shifts how they think.

As a young teacher, I was assigned to teach music to grade seven and eight students in an inner city Chicago school. I had studied music and music education in university, and had some expertise. That first year, I assumed the role of an expert who had knowledge my students were supposed to have. It was an utter disaster. My knowledge was irrelevant to their lives. They expressed that over and over again in disruptive behavior. My biggest frustration was that they learned nothing from all my efforts. The next year I began the year with a focused conversation about what my students needed from my class to get what they needed in their own lives. Building on their needs, I created a Black music history course that satisfied the curriculum and taught the reading skills and self-esteem that they so desperately wanted. My expertise was tapped and shared when appropriate, and so was the experience of the students. The students were amazingly attentive and engaged. Not only did the students learn about music, they learned that they had important wisdom and experience, and their confidence carried over into other learning. I learned a huge amount about the history of music, and about my students' lives. Through this experience I let go of having to know the answers and learned to facilitate learning. Those years remain a highlight of my teaching career.

Separation of the teacher's two roles: to present information and to facilitate information processing is key to generating the hunger for knowledge in the students.

Maintaining an open stance in facilitating learning is an important part of the learning process. John Kloepfer, in *The Art of Formative Questioning: A Way to Foster Self-Disclosure* says:

> A primary quality of the facilitator asking questions is his openness, or what Socrates called *docta ignorantia*. While the facilitator is a skilled methodologian (the "*docta*" part of that famous phrase), he professes an ignorance—*ignorantia*—a not knowing, an extreme openness to whatever comes forth from the conversation. However, false conversations use the conversation simply to prove a currently held position — they lack the genuine openness required for true insight to emerge.

Many of us who are teachers or trainers have developed a real habit of intervention. We have been trained to correct, amplify, or amend what has been said. A focused conversation has no content to teach. This means that the teacher is required to stand in the "not knowing" required for openness while he or she is leading the conversation. When the teacher uses a conversation to ferret out the hidden answers that they already know many students simply will not participate. They will shut down and wait for the teacher to tell them, rather than risk being wrong. They will only learn to parrot back the teacher's answers on the exam, and will rarely connect the information with their own lives.

Two students I know well have very different learning styles. One is very verbal, confident and assertive. The other is quiet and introverted. Both reacted to a high school English teacher who insisted there was only his way to interpret the meaning of the play, Hamlet. The quiet student never participated in class discussions, fearing to have the wrong answers and be publicly rebuked. The verbal one guessed the answers the teacher wanted and said them out loud to impress the teacher, though he yearned to explore other possibilities in a real discussion. Both spent an inordinate amount of anxious energy trying to guess what the teacher wanted on the exam. No energy was spent on developing their own critical thinking, and for both, the lessons of Hamlet remained irrelevant.

I learned the hard way that adults as well as young students react angrily when they believe a teacher is trying to manipulate them to her own ideas through a conversation. Once I was teaching a group of educators how to set up school-community partnerships. I gave an impassioned speech in which I presented some underlying principles of participation. I followed that with facilitating a conversation on their response to my speech. The whole group was convinced that I was trying to manipulate them to my "right answers" that I had just extolled in my speech. They became extraordinarily offended, and negated all the points I had made instead of exploring ways to implement them.

Part of preparation for leading a conversation is to develop a real curiosity about what the group might know—the opposite of hoping against hope that they come up with "right" answers—that is, those that agree with the views of the facilitator. This might mean repeating to oneself before starting the conversation, "I wonder what new insight the group will come up with today?" This applies as much to students as it does to fellow adults. Young children often bring a fresh perspective from their own experience that allows everyone to see new insights.

When the teacher has a body of facts to impart, they are best shared through a presentation. There are examples in Chapter 1 and Chapter 10 on how to make a clear presentation using the four levels of the process. It may be useful to combine the presentation with a focused conversation or two. If the teacher is an expert on Browning's poetry, she may want to start by leading a focused conversation with the students on the body of Browning's work to determine where their concerns and difficulties lie. Then she can focus her presentation accordingly to their level of experience, and not waste time either telling the group something they already know, or assuming a high level of knowledge and going over their heads. After the presentation, she might lead another conversation to integrate their learning from the lecture and apply it to their own writing.

In such cases, where presentation and reflection are combined, it is critical to separate the roles of presenter and the role of conversation facilitator. If it is not possible to have different people play these roles, as is often the case in a classroom, the presenter should avoid slipping into the "expert" role while leading group reflection. Something as simple as changing between a "presenter" hat and a "facilitator" hat can make a huge difference in the effect of the conversation. Sometimes putting the questions on a flipchart or chalkboard detaches the person and their opinions from the process.

Sometimes letting go of having all the right answers is disorienting or downright frightening to a teacher. My experience is that when I do this successfully, I learn from my students without losing my teaching role, and I gain respect from my students. After many years of experience and a few insightful movies (such as *The Dead Poets Society*), a really important insight came to me — if you ask people for their wisdom, and really listen to it, they think you are wise. The real secret is that if you ask people for their wisdom and really listen to it, you become wiser! Through the group discussion, the students also realize how much they know collectively, and how well they can solve problems when they put their minds together.

Following the guidelines above will help you facilitate learning and thoughtful decision-making, whether it is with a class or a group of adults.

WHY DIDN'T MY CONVERSATION WORK? AND WHAT TO DO ABOUT IT

Even with a good method, solid preparation, and willing participants, not every conversation will go well. Rather than write off the experience as "something that I can't do", it is helpful to reflect on what happened and why. Such reflection turns difficulty into a learning experience.

The following table, compiled from extensive experience, is a general guide to what can go wrong in a conversation, and some possible strategies to try to deal with them. Some of these apply to classrooms, and some are more typical of meetings with staff or parents. Of course, they do not cover all communication problems. Each situation is unique with different participants, different topics, and different issues. If your conversation runs into trouble, conduct a private conversation with yourself about what happened, using the table to help you think through the problems you discover.

Commonly Reported Troubles	Possible Reasons	Possible Solutions
1. Group isn't focusing	Chaotic or inhospitable setting	Rearrange space to ensure a quiet setting where participants are seated so they can see each other.
	Never really getting the group's attention	Plan an informal time while people are gathering, but limit it.
		Respectfully call for the group's attention to begin the conversation.
		Start on time to encourage taking each other seriously.
	Context not clear	In the context, say enough about the purpose of the meeting and the method so the group feels free to participate.
	Topic not relevant to group	Take more time in the planning stage to think through what the group needs.
2. Group doesn't respond to questions	Weak rapport with the facilitator or the group distrusts the facilitator	Speak opening words with warmth and an honouring style.
		Look at people and really listen to them.
		In your opening context, explain that as a facilitator, you are there to elicit the group's best thinking, and you have no answers.
		Start with an introductory conversation where you ask each person their name and what they want from this conversation, then ask them to draw out the mandate the whole group is giving you.
	The topic is out of focus	Clarify the specific aims of the conversation, and how the conversation is relevant
	Abstract beginning point, e.g. "Let's talk about assessment. What does it mean?"	Clarify a concrete beginning point that the group shares, e.g. the school's present report cards, or a policy document
		Make objective questions more clear and concrete
	Questions are out of order and are disrupting the natural thinking process	Check the level of the question, say, "oops, I meant to ask a different question," or "hang on, let me ask this first," and then substitute another question.

Commonly Reported Troubles	Possible Reasons	Possible Solutions
2. Group doesn't respond to questions (continued)	Questions are not open-ended; group senses it is being led towards a conclusion not its own	Rephrase question in an open-ended way in *Jeopardy* style — "What is..."
	Questions are moving too fast; or moving too slow — like beads on a string.	Note where the group is, drop or add questions that will help the group get the information it needs and arrive at the decision point.
	Many people prefer to be silent in the large group	Ask for "someone who hasn't said anything for awhile", or call by name — "Ali, what are you thinking?" Judiciously use small groups.
	People don't feel safe in the group (an authority figure such as the teacher or principal present, etc.)	Change the overall composition of the group: break the group up into smaller groups of like people until they are more confident.
	People shy	Go around the group on the first objective question or so to get everyone's voice out on something safe to build confidence.
	Situation too formal	Try changing the setting to be more informal, such as sitting down.
	Group is allergic to "touchy-feely stuff"	Ask reflective level questions with care so that people do not have to use feeling words to answer: for example, "what part of this upset you the most?" or "what immediate associations did you have with this?" (but do not leave out the reflective level altogether)

Commonly Reported Troubles	Possible Reasons	Possible Solutions
3. Group gives wrong answers	You have a hidden agenda — you think there is one right answer	Remind yourself that you have your facilitator hat on and you want the group's wisdom.
		or
		Stop asking questions and make a presentation.
	Questions are not in the right order	Check the level of question, say "Hang on, let me ask this first", and substitute another question.
		Rephrase the question more clearly to focus the level of answer.
	The question is not sufficiently clear or focused	If the group trusts that you really want their answers, you might give a sample answer to your question to give them an idea of what you are looking for.
		With younger students, give a wide range of possible answers for them to choose from to spark their understanding.
4. Group is not answering with real answers	Members of the group feel unsafe; the group is not ready to participate	Try less personal conversation topics until the group is confident they will be taken seriously and/or can take responsibility for the results.
	Questions are not specific enough	Test questions in advance by imagining how the group might answer, or try them on someone.
	Participants have hidden agenda. See above: #2.	Ask specific questions to give the opportunity for hidden agenda items to become explicit.

Commonly Reported Troubles	Possible Reasons	Possible Solutions
5. Some participants dominate	Perhaps they don't feel they have been heard (yes, even if the group can't believe this).	Listen seriously, demonstrate "hearing them" by writing, or active listening, and respectfully cutting off — "I think we've got your main point. I'd love to hear more at the break. Now, somebody else."
	The leader who is charged with responsibility for the outcome doesn't trust the group	Take the leader aside, check for concerns, let him know what his choices are and the consequences of dominating; address his concerns in the process.
	Conversation style may be too open	Go around the room on a few questions. Ask each person to respond succinctly.
	Imbalance between people who are quiet, and those who love to express in a group.	Use small groups, mixing quiet and expressive together, then have groups report their results to the larger group.
6. Group goes off on tangents	Group wants to escape topic or responsibility	Reflect with the group about what's happening (use a focused conversation).
	Topic is unfocused, or deemed irrelevant	Respectfully, but firmly, bring the group back to the subject. Refocus the context and the questions (See also: 1. "Group Isn't Focusing")
	Facilitator is too wishy-washy	Remind yourself that facilitating is not about being liked, but about getting the group to handle its concerns. (See also: 1. "Group Isn't Focusing")
7. Not getting useful results	Topic not deemed relevant by group	See above: 1. "Group Isn't Focusing".
	Topic is too big to be dealt with adequately in one conversation	Design several conversations on different parts of the topic.
	Questions are not getting out useful information	Check prepared questions. Work backward from needed result to what data is needed at each level.

Commonly Reported Troubles	Possible Reasons	Possible Solutions
8. Arguments break out	Context of respect for each other's views not established, or people are unaware of ways to hear each other.	Establish strong context of multi-dimensional reality: "we all see facets of the whole diamond".
		Intervene respectfully—let the first person finish, then ask, "Now what is your perspective on this?" Then invite someone else's response.
		Ask: "What are the underlying patterns under these conflicting responses?"
	Facilitator is showing bias	Check yourself to see whether you are receiving all answers.
		Remind yourself: "I am curious."
	Students want to impress the teacher with their ability to argue a point	Remind students that they aren't getting points for arguing, but for thoughtful listening and participation.
9. Group challenges the facilitator	Facilitator is not conveying self-confidence	Let people know at the beginning that you are using a carefully thought-through process, and you are not pushing any answers.
	Facilitator conveys mixed messages of expert and questioner	Check your questions to ensure open-endedness.
	Group over-sensitive to the facilitator's power	Separate the roles of expert presenter and questioner by writing the questions in a visible place, or by asking someone else to lead the conversation.

Part III

Focused Conversations

Introduction

Any activity that requires higher order thinking and reasoning is likely to
result in more transfer of knowledge to long-term memory and incorporation
into memory in meaningful ways.
David Carter-Todd

The following conversations have been designed for real-life situations in classrooms and schools. They were designed by active teachers and educators in several countries. Each was carefully edited to make it applicable to a variety of similar situations. They are intended as templates that will make it easy for you to use the Focused Conversation method in your classroom, school, or parent meeting.

The conversations are arranged in five chapters, each focusing on a broad category of common topics. Within chapters six to nine, they are further sub-divided into expected participants – students, teachers and staff members, or parents and community members.

Chapter 6. Making Learning Meaningful

The examples in this chapter provide ways to solve the problems of teaching clear thinking, facilitating the capacity to think abstractly and probe meaning, and providing a logical structure to present information. They also address the motivation of students to learn and the problem of applying and making use of what is learned.

Chapter 7. Making Communication Effective in Groups

Examples are provided of conversations for student group projects, staff meetings, and parent councils which foster timely and effective communication, build shared understanding and respect, and allow a group of people to come to wise decisions.

Chapter 8. Preventing and Solving Problems

These conversations demonstrate how the conversation method can be used by students, teachers, administrators, and parents to resolve misunderstandings and conflicts and resolve difficult problems, in one-on-one and group situations.

Chapter 9. Evaluating Learning

The examples in this chapter provide conversations for self-evaluation, as well as evaluating performance and accomplishments of both students and staff in an effective and fair manner that allows for growth.

Chapter 10. Creative Applications

In this chapter are some specific examples of creative applications of the four-level process. There are sets of conversations that work together to enhance learning, and other unique, creative applications of the four steps of the process.

How to find a helpful conversation template

Topics of interest: The list of conversation topics in the table of contents may spark applications that you will find helpful. If you already have a topic in mind, scan the table of contents or use the index to find a related conversation. Occasionally a conversation can be used directly from the book, with a few modifications. Most of the time, however, the structure of a conversation in the book will give you ideas to create your own conversation.

Conversations designed for your audience: Look for similar conversations for more than one audience for clues to adapting the questions to your audience. For example, a conversation for grade seven students on a movie might incorporate some questions from the conversation on a puppet show for second-graders as well as some of the questions on a movie for teachers.

Similar starting points: Sometimes there are several conversations on a similar topic that have differing beginning points. If you want to have a conversation on parent councils, for example, there is one that focuses on a mandated policy, and another that begins with parents' experiences with other parent groups. Try the one whose starting point is closer to yours.

Similar aims and objectives: Sometimes the kind of outcome you want is more a more important similarity to look for in a sample conversation than the topic. For example, if you want recommendations for responding to a policy, the topic of the policy does not affect the questions very much. The questions explore the significance of whatever policy you are focusing on, and bring out the group's recommendations.

Using the preparation form

When you find a template or set of templates you can use, turn to the Focused Conversation preparation form in the Appendix. Use the instructions in Chapter Four to plan your own aims, opening, closing, and questions, copying the appropriate parts from the templates. Don't forget to test your conversation by imagining your group answering the questions you have written. You may well need to adapt parts to fit the language or style of your group.

CHAPTER 6

Making Learning Meaningful

The conversations in this chapter are designed to deepen learning and help students and adults apply it to their lives.

Some of the model conversations are designed to help students — to understand assignments, to explore the deeper meaning of a topic, or to relate learning to real life applications.

Other conversations are to help teachers and parents — to reflect on events and activities, to draw out insight, and to explore new views or ideas.

Reflecting on a Field Trip to the Zoo

Designed for
Students – Elementary

Situation
A class of first grade students has returned from a field trip to the zoo. They sit in a circle on the rug for a quick conversation.

Rational Aim
To remember the many kinds of animals they saw.

Experiential Aim
To experience appreciation of themselves and the world.

The Conversation

Opening

Let's discuss our trip to the zoo.

Objective Questions

What animals did you see?

Reflective Questions

What was your favorite animal? Why?

Interpretive Questions

What are some similarities between children and animals? Differences?

Why was this a good trip?

Decisional Questions

What animals would you like to see again?

What animal would you like to learn more about?

Closing

Draw your favorite animal and we will hang the pictures on a zoo mural outside the classroom.

Learning from a Puppet Show

Designed for
Students – Elementary

Situation
A class of second grade students has gone on a field trip to a puppet show of *Rumplestiltskin* at the theater. Afterward they sit in a circle to talk about the play.

Rational Aim
To have the students remember the story of *Rumplestiltskin* and to learn about honesty.

Experiential Aim
To experience the fun of watching puppets tell a story. To be reflective about their own lives.

The Conversation

Opening

Let's think about how the puppet show ended.

Objective Questions

Who were the characters?

What costumes did they wear?

What scenes do you remember?

What were some of the lines you heard?

Reflective Questions

Where were you excited?

When did you want to cheer?

Where did you become afraid?

Interpretive Questions

What did you learn about honesty?

What did you learn about making promises you can't keep?

Decisional Questions

What can you do to remind yourself about being honest?

Reflecting on a Story about Self-image

Designed for
Students – Elementary

Situation
Third grade students are studying a story in reading class called *The Golden Eagle*. The teacher wants the students to understand their reading, but also to use the message in the literature to change their own lives.

Rational Aim
To understand that you are what you believe you are.

Experiential Aim
To no longer be stuck in an old image of one's self.

The Conversation

Opening

Let's read the story of *The Golden Eagle* out loud.

Objective Questions

What words or phrases do you remember?

What characters were in the story?

What were some pictures that came to mind as you heard the story?

What were some of the differences between the chicken and the eagle that the story pointed out?

Reflective Questions

What emotions did you experience, for example, scared, happy, sad, or safe?

What character seemed a lot like you?

What did this story remind you of — things that have happened to you, things in school, things at home, things from stories or TV or movies?

Interpretive Questions

How did the eagle feel about himself? Why?

How did the chicken feel? Why?

How did what they believed affect who they were?

What was the message of the story?

Decisional Questions

What would you want to change in your life after hearing the story?

Closing

Whenever you find you are getting stuck, close your eyes for a moment, and imagine yourself as a golden eagle. See what difference it makes.

Reflecting on a Story—An Alternative Point of View

Designed for
Students – Elementary

Situation
Students in a grade two class are listening to an alternative version of a fairy tale, and the teacher would like them to discuss the messages in the story.

Rational Aim
To understand the story and learn about alternative points of view on a story.

Experiential Aim
To be able to question points of view when given other stories.

Hints
You could follow this conversation with a writing assignment where students rewrite another fairy tale or a familiar story from one or more alternative viewpoints.

The Conversation

Opening

Class, today we are going to listen to a story — a fairy tale. There is something different about this story. We've already heard another version of this story. Let's listen, and then we are going to talk about it. *(Read the story.)*

Objective Questions

Who were the characters in this story?

What happened at the beginning of the story? The middle? The end?

Reflective Questions

Which character did you like the best?

What part of the story did you laugh at?

Have you ever had a situation where no one listened to your version of what happened?

Give an example. How did you feel?

Interpretive Questions

Why did you like the character you liked?

What was the story about?

How was this story different from the usual version of the fairy tale?

Why do you think the wolf wrote this story?

Decisional Questions

What have you learned from this version of the story?

What will you think about the next time you read a story?

Closing

A story sometimes has two or even more sides.

Reflecting on a Story about Something That is Not What it Seems

Designed for
Students – Elementary

Situation
A sixth grade class has just read a short story where the sound of a monster in the fog turned out to be something ordinary and familiar.

Rational Aim
To introduce students to a short story and have them discuss the merits of the story.

Experiential Aim
To experience that the unknown is not always something to fear.

The Conversation

Opening

Let's see what this story can tell us.

Objective Questions

Where does the story take place?

Who are the main characters?

What happens first? Then? After that?

Reflective Questions

What images came to your mind as I read the story?

What part was scary?

What did you find funny?

Who did you identify with?

Interpretive Questions

Where have you experienced something like this?

How would you talk about what a monster is?

What do you think the author was trying to get across to the readers?

What makes those important messages?

Decisional Questions

How has this story changed you, or your thinking?

Closing

Your homework assignment is to write a short story about something or someone who is not what they seem at first.

Responding to a Play

Designed for
Students – Elementary

Situation
A group of children with a wide range of ages has gone to see a live presentation of *Peter Pan*. Some think it's "baby stuff."

Rational Aim
To recall facts, gather new ideas and use higher-level thinking skills.

Experiential Aim
To respect each other's insights.

The Conversation

Opening

Let's reflect on what we saw at the play.

Objective Questions

What's one thing you saw or heard in the play?

Who were the characters?

What were the events in the story? What happened? Where did they go? What did they do?

Reflective Questions

How did you feel when Peter Pan flew through the air?

What was a scary part of the play?

What part did you laugh at?

Interpretive Questions

How did Peter and Wendy feel about each other?

How did they feel about the other children?

What act would you interpret as an act of love?

What act would you interpret as hate?

Why did Captain Hook act like he did?

Why did Peter do what he did?

If you were in this story, who would you be? Why?

Decisional Questions

What was this story all about?

If you had to write another ending to this story, what would you write?

What would you name this story, in your own words?

Closing

Peter Pan is a play for all age levels. We can all learn something from it.

Extending a Math Exercise in Elementary School

Designed for
Students – Elementary

Situation
The teacher has just involved the children in an exercise manipulating toothpicks to show first 2 + 2 and the total number, then groups of 2 and the total number; then 3 + 3 and the total number, and two groups of 3 and the total number. Students leave the groupings on their desks in front of them.

Rational Aim
To understand that multiplication is a shortcut for addition — that "times" means "groups of".

Experiential Aim
To realize "Aha! I can do this!"

The Conversation

Opening

We're going to see what we can learn from what we just did.

Objective Questions

Describe what you see on your desk.

Reflective Questions

What surprises you?

Interpretive Questions

How would you describe the pattern you see?

What have you discovered?

How is multiplying similar to adding? How is it different?

Why do you think the total of 3 + 3 is the same as the total of 2 groups of 3?

This is how we can write this: $3 + 3 = 6$, or $3 \times 2 = 6$

Decisional Questions

How would you summarize what you see on your desk? Answer by drawing it and write the math sentences beneath your pictures.

Try again with 4 + 4 + 4 and 3 groups of 4, first with the toothpicks, then drawing them.

Write this in two ways.

Try it first alone, then we'll do it together.

Closing

Wow! You're doing multiplication! Whenever you do "a number of groups of" a number of things, you're doing multiplication.

Hand out assignment sheet for homework, extending the exercise.

Integrating the Experience of the Day

Designed for
Students – Elementary

Situation
In an elementary classroom, a teacher reflects with her class daily at the end of the day.

Rational Aim
To create a deeper understanding of the implications of the day.
To be conscious of learning from experiences.

Experiential Aim
To experience the day as complete.
To be affirmed in the day's challenges.

Hints
There are lots of questions here. Usually you ask only one or two questions at each level, depending on time and flow.

Other Applications
Solitary conversation for journaling.
End of session, a unit of work, or term.
Daily debriefing for a group on a work/study tour to another culture.

The Conversation

Opening

Just before the bell rings, let's wind up the day with a quick reflection.

Objective Questions

What is something that happened today — in class or on the playground?

What is something you saw?

What is something someone said?

What are some sounds you heard?

Reflective Questions

What was something funny, or something sad that you experienced today?

What made you excited or frustrated?

What were some of the feelings you saw others having today?

Interpretive Questions

Where did you experience something that went really well today?

What did not go so well for you?

What was really appropriate behavior?

What was really inappropriate behavior?

What was something that didn't happen today that you wanted to have happen?

Where did you see learning happening today?

Where did you see someone's needs being met?

Where did you have a breakthrough?

Where did you achieve something in spite of the problems?

Where did you experience individual success?

Where did you see a real team effort?

What would you say this class was about today?

Decisional Questions

What would you have changed about today if you could?

What would you have kept the same?

(continued)

Integrating the Experience of the Day *(continued)*

If you could take away everything from this day except one event or experience, which event or experience would that be?

If you had to explain to somebody from "outer space" what you did today, what would you say?

How would you draw a picture of this day?

What rating between 1 and 10 would you give to how good this day was for you?

What name would you give to this day? "This was the day of..."

What do you need to do as a result of this day?

What changes can you make for tomorrow? Next week?

Closing

Thanks for sharing your reflections about the day. A lot happened in a few short hours. I've learned a lot from what you have said.

Using a Televised Sportscast to Teach Teamwork

Designed for
Students – Elementary

Situation
A middle-school boys' gym class is preparing for an upcoming intramural "Olympics".

Rational Aim
To remember the importance of team play.

Experiential Aim
To experience appreciation of self and world.

Hints
You can adjust these questions to focus on any particular sport, event or game.

aThe Conversation

Opening

Let's discuss the teamwork in last night's basketball game. How many of you saw the game?

Objective Questions

What plays do you remember from last night's game?

How many points did each player score?

What happened after a key player was fouled?

Reflective Questions

What did you like best about the game?

What did you like the least?

Interpretive Questions

How did each player in the game contribute to winning the game?

How did players who sat on the bench through the whole game contribute?

What kinds of teamwork did you see going on?

What would you have done differently to make the teamwork stronger?

What does it take to win?

Decisional Questions

What does this tell you about preparing to be a team in our upcoming Olympics?

Preparing for Writing an Exam Essay Question

Designed for
Students – Elementary

Situation
A grade eight student has been given an essay assignment on an exam and needs to think through quickly what she knows about the topic before starting to write.

Rational Aim
To have a focused list of key points to write about on the exam.

Experiential Aim
To have the confidence needed to write well.

The Conversation

Opening
OK, I can do this!

Objective Questions
What facts do I remember about this topic?

What have the teachers or the books said?

Reflective Questions
What is most interesting about this?

What part am I most confident about?

What questions do I have?

Interpretive Questions
What do I think is important about this topic?

Or

Why is this important?

What do I think it means?

Decisional Questions
What key points shall I make?

What comes first?

Or

How do I organize these ideas?

Closing
OK, here goes.

Finding Meaning in a Popular Film

Designed for
Students – High School

Situation
A grade nine English class is watching a popular film as part of a unit on media literacy. The teacher introduces the concept of media literacy, and introduces the film.

Rational Aim
To understand the deeper meaning of a popular film

Experiential Aim
Experience the "aha" of delving beneath the surface of a film.

The Conversation

Opening

Now that we've seen the film, we're going to use a focused conversation to probe the meaning beneath the surface of the film. We will take about half an hour.

Objective Questions

What characters and faces do you recall?

What is one scene you remember?

What lines of dialogue, words and phrases do you recall?

What sounds did you notice?

Reflective Questions

What emotions did you see in the film?

What emotions did you experience while watching the film?

Where were you surprised or uneasy?

Where were you reminded of something in your own life?

What or who did you identify with in the film? Why?

Interpretive Questions

What ideas caught your attention?

What do you think the director was trying to say?

From your experience, where was this film right on target?

Where would you say, this is really off the mark?

What messages is the film trying to communicate?

What can we learn from this film?

Decisional Questions

What might you do differently as a result of seeing this film?

Who would you like to show this film to?

Closing

It has been said that the best films give us a window into our own real lives. I think we have seen how this might be the case.

Exploring the Meaning of a Work of Art

Designed for
Students – High School

Situation
A high school art teacher has students studying paintings by the great masters. In one of the paintings there are visual clues to the culture of the time that can lead to some insights on racism.

Rational Aim
To understand the cultural context of the painter, and to see how it affects his work.

Experiential Aim
To experience the impact of the work on students' own lives.

Hints
Questions will need to be thought through very carefully in relation to the specific work of art. A conversation of a Pieter Breughel painting with lots of people and action is vastly different than a conversation on a Tom Thompson landscape, etc.

The Conversation

Opening

Let's focus on this painting for a while. There may just be some interesting messages hidden in this picture.

Objective Questions

What objects do you see in this picture?

What people or characters do you see?

What are the different characters wearing?

What are they doing?

What are they surrounded by?

What do you notice about the size of the characters as they are painted?

What directions are they facing in the painting?

Reflective Questions

Which character do you find your eyes returning to the most?

Which character do you like the most?

Which people do you dislike or not notice much?

What does the way this scene is painted remind you of?

Interpretive Questions

Why do you think the painter painted the characters in this way?

What message was he trying to get across? Why?

If this were a picture of today's world, how would it look?

What would be the same? What would be different?

If you were in this picture, who would you be and what would you be doing?

Decisional Questions

How would you summarize the meaning of this painting for today's world?

What is its meaning for you?

What will you do differently as a result of what you have learned today?

Closing

The meaning of art is in the interpretation by the viewer. When we take seriously the work of an artist, it can give us insight into both the artist and our own lives.

Thinking through Issues in a Documentary Video

Designed for
Students – High School

Situation
A grade twelve World Issues class is viewing a documentary video on homelessness.

Rational Aim
To know some of the basic issues related to our unit of study.

Experiential Aim
To experience a desire to act on the concerns of this video.

The Conversation

Opening

We want to see a video today, and then reflect together on what we saw and heard. Here is the video I would like you to watch

Now, we want to share our responses to the film.

Objective Questions

What visual pictures stood out?

What words or phrases caught your attention? What colors? Sounds?

What characters do you recall?

Now let's rehearse together the basic story of the video. What happened first? After that?

Reflective Questions

Where did you get caught up in this story?

Where did you get intrigued or fascinated?

Where were you irritated or angry?

What other feelings did you experience?

What other associations, events, or experiences came to mind?

What memories did it trigger?

Interpretive Questions

What are the main points of the video?

What are some of the root issues portrayed?

Which of these issues concern you the most?

Decisional Questions

What practical steps could you take to meet this issue?

As a class, what practical actions could we take?

What might we do in the next couple of weeks to begin to implement these actions?

What is your personal commitment to action?

Closing

Well, let's stop here, although we could continue this conversation for a long time. This is great. We have begun to think both concretely and personally about a serious issue.

Understanding the Movie *Schindler's List*

Designed for
Students – High School

Situation
About 100 high school juniors and seniors from an urban public high school have watched the movie *Schindler's List*, directed by Steven Spielberg. The students represent ethnically diverse backgrounds but no specific subject area of studies (i.e., this isn't a history class). Students are familiar with the Focused Conversation method.

Rational Aim
To immerse students in World War II history and the challenges of that time.
To ground the difference one life can make, using Hitler and Schindler as examples.
To influence students to decide not to allow events like these to be repeated.
To have students understand that:
• A person's operating images are important.
• It is possible for a human being to have unbridled, uncontrollable hatred.
• Group unconsciousness can have tragic consequences.

Experiential Aim
To have students experience the horror of the holocaust, the reality of a war mentality, and the struggle of hard choices (between wrong and wrong).
To appreciate Schindler's strategy to help those in the camps.

The Conversation

Opening

This is a debriefing conversation. We will be using the Focused Conversation method. Answer each question briefly, and answer only the questions asked. Everyone is expected to participate, so listen to each other's responses. No speeches will be allowed!

Objective Questions

Let's begin by briefly reconstructing the essential facts. The year was 1939. In what country did this take place? What other historical facts were given?

What were the names of the characters? Who have we left out?

What scenes do you recall?

What lines of dialogue do you recall?

What sounds did you hear?

What objects did you see?

What statistical facts were shared?

Reflective Questions

Did you laugh at all during the movie? When?

When did you feel like crying?

When were you afraid? Experience terror?

When did you experience relief?

When did you want to jump up and help?

If you could edit out one scene, which one would it be?

What would you like to add?

When did you first realize the situation was out of control?

When did the Jews first realize it? (When did they realize that this was beyond hassling them and annihilation was intended?)

Interpretive Questions

Let's talk about the man, Schindler just a bit. What else do we know about Schindler?

What kind of man was Schindler?

What values did he hold? What values did other characters — pick one or two — hold? How were Schindler's values unique?

(continued)

Understanding the Movie *Schindler's List (continued)*

Hints

This conversation will take about an hour, with 15 to 20 minutes for the objective and interpretive levels, and 10 minutes each for the reflective and decisional levels.

At the objective level, push the group for a significant number of responses to each question.

In the middle of the reflective questions, with the shift to focusing on Schindler, the conversation does a contextual "re-wind" in which specific objective and reflective level comments are repeated and reexamined in order to dig deeper. Restate quickly any objective level comments about Schindler, particularly the scenes already shared in which he was the key player. Encourage a diversity of different answers at the reflective and interpretive levels, and class discussion of those answers.

Which side was he on, exactly?

Do you like him? Why or why not?

When did you notice changes in his attitude?

What is a specific scene or line of dialogue where you saw this?

What choices did he have?

What did he eventually give up? What did he get back?

What did he accomplish in the end?

What kept the Nazis from getting him?

How could all this have happened?

Where in the world today is harassment of specific ethnic or religious groups going on? What makes these examples serious concerns for us and our society?

Decisional Questions

What have you learned from this film?

What do you suppose Schindler told his grandchildren never to forget?

What do you suppose those on *Schindler's List* told their grandchildren never to forget?

How can we avoid repeating the negative aspects of our history?

How are you a different person because you saw *Schindler's List*?

Closing

Well, as you see, history is our shared experience, and we are learning as we go along. Thank you for your wisdom and insight. The assignment is to write a 300-word essay on a specific way to overcome racial and ethnic hatred.

Understanding a High School Math Concept

Designed for
Students – High School

Situation
The math teacher has just demonstrated a complicated equation and its solution on the board. The class looks mostly blank.

Rational Aim
To understand the complex concepts and steps of the math topic.

Experiential Aim
To feel involved and respected for participating
To take increased responsibility for their own learning.

Hints
As a teaching conversation, this is one of the most difficult to refrain from having all the answers as the teacher. Remind yourself that what students discover themselves will be learned more thoroughly than what they merely hear from someone else. Help with answers only when no one can answer, or when you can see that your words will clarify thinking the students are struggling to articulate.

The Conversation

Opening
Let's discuss this problem to make sure we all understand it.

Objective Questions
First let's recap the steps. What did we do? I'll write them as you say them.

What was given?

What steps did I go through? First? Second? Next?

Reflective Questions
What part was most confusing? Simplest? Hardest?

Interpretive Questions
How is this similar to the equation we did in our last class? How is it different?

How can this equation be used – At home? In carpentry? In business? In engineering? Etc.

Decisional Questions
What do you need to do to master this process?

Closing
Your assignment for next class is…(based on what the students have said they need).

Reflecting on a Team Experiential Learning Exercise

Designed for
Students – High School

Situation
A group of high school students is preparing for a cooperative learning assignment. The group breaks up into small teams of four to six people to do an experiential learning exercise. Each team forms a circle and gets five minutes to tear an animal from a newspaper, working as a team. The newspaper is passed around, and each team member can make one straight tear. A team member can make sounds or expressions of the animal, but during the first two rounds of tearing, no one may talk.

Rational Aim
To learn how to get to a good result through teamwork.

Experiential Aim
To experience that teamwork is dynamical, and that energy, determination, and communication are needed to get to a good result.

Hints
This conversation can be adapted easily to any team building exercise.

The Conversation

Opening

You have just performed a teamwork exercise. Let's take a few minutes to talk about what happened.

Objective Questions

What animal(s) did you make?

What sounds did you hear?

What scenes do you remember while we were working?

What words or phrases did you hear people say?

What emotions did you observe in the group?

Reflective Questions

Where did you feel excited during the exercise?

What was frustrating?

What situations or events does this exercise remind you of?

Interpretive Questions

Which things did your team do that helped reach the end result?

What did you miss in the team process?

How could you improve the teamwork?

What did you learn from this exercise?

Decisional Questions

How can we use these ideas in our teamwork assignments?

What's something new or different you'll do in your work or life after doing this exercise?

Closing

It's interesting to see how this exercise is always different, with new perspectives and teamwork. Thanks for your cooperation and input.

Evaluating of a Video on Violence in Society

Designed for
Students – High School

Situation
A high school teacher wants input from students on whether or not a video on violence in society will be useful to use in a lower grade classroom.

Rational Aim
To get feedback from students on a video on violence in society.

Experiential Aim
To experience that all ideas are heard and respected.

The Conversation

Opening

The principal asked me to evaluate this video for use with first year students. I want your input for that evaluation, to know how you think it might affect them. First let's watch the video.

Objective Questions

What words or phrases do you recall from the video?

What were the main points made by the speaker?

Reflective Questions

What was your first reaction to this video?

What did you think was interesting?

What frustrated you?

Interpretive Questions

What are some of the root issues?

How do first year students experience these issues?

Which issues have implications for our high school?

What might be the effects of this video on first year students?

Decisional Questions

What are your recommendations about the video?

How can we use it? Should we use it?

Closing

These are the suggestions I hear you making….

Thank you for your input.

I will pass your opinions on to the principal, along with my own reflections.

Reflecting on a Group Experience

Designed for
Students – High School

Situation
A group of young people has participated in an unusual kinesthetic experience called "The Dance of Peace." Some were reluctant participants; others were deeply moved. After lunch, the trainer is leading the group in a debriefing of their experience.

Rational Aim
To clarify what we did.
To discover common motifs and themes.
To identify the cultural origins of dance patterns.

Experiential Aim
To experience the wonder of each culture's contribution, and to feel the exhilaration of the dance.

Other Applications
You can debrief after any experiential learning exercise, e.g., a rope course, using similar questions.

The Conversation

Opening
Think back to the dancing we did this morning.

Objective Questions
What movements do you remember?
What did the movement look like?
What dances did we do?
What sounds do you recall? What instruments were used?

Reflective Questions
How did you feel as you were dancing?
At what point did you feel unsure, confused, or embarrassed?
At what point did you feel excited, deeply moved, or peaceful?
When did you really "get into it"?
Where have you seen or experienced something similar?
What did this remind you of?

Interpretive Questions
What was going on in this dance?
Why do you think the creator of these dances created them?
What were they trying to express of communicate?
What kind of experiences were they trying to provide for people?
What can we learn from these dances?
How were you changed by this experience?

Decisional Questions
To whom would you like to teach these dances?
Where would you like to see them used again?
Whom do you wish had been here this morning?

Closing
When we started, I felt silly. After it was over, I thought, "This was fantastic."

Understanding an Assignment

Designed for
Students – High School

Situation
High school students are given a verbal assignment for individual projects in carpentry class, for which there is the possibility for creative adaptation. Each student has to pick a project he or she intends to carry out. This conversation takes place inside a student's head as he or she thinks about what they would like to do.

Rational Aim
To clarify an assignment and have a plan for doing it.

Experiential Aim
To be motivated to do the assignment.

Hints
The teacher may put these questions on the board or on a worksheet to guide the students' thinking.

The Conversation

Opening
I guess it's up to me to choose exactly what project I want to do.

Objective Questions
What words did the teacher say?

What did he say we can do?

What did he say we can't do?

Reflective Questions
What do I like about this assignment?

What do I dislike about this assignment?

What am I interested in that this reminds me of?

Interpretive Questions
What possibilities are there?

What's the purpose of this assignment?

What can I make that will be beautiful or useful?

What skills might I learn from doing this?

Decisional Questions
What shall I make for my project?

What will I do to carry out this assignment?

Closing
I'll tell the teacher what I plan to do.

Practicing English by Reviewing TV Habits

Designed for
Students – Adult

Situation
An ESL class is studying words that have to do with TV. After the opening, the class breaks into small groups for discussion. The questions are written out on paper for each group.

Rational Aim
To practice English language by reviewing TV habits.

Experiential Aim
To have fun practicing English with a minimum of stress on a topic of student interest.

Hints
Carefully choose your questions so that the answers help students practice the grammar and new vocabulary you have been studying.

The Conversation

Opening

For our regular weekly topical narrative, let's review our new TV-related words and phrases.

Then we're going to have conversations in small groups about our television watching to practice the words.

On this paper are the questions for you to ask and answer.

Objective Questions

How many hours of television do you watch most weeks?

What TV programs do you watch? (For example, sports, news, action, or music)

How long do you watch TV at one time?

Reflective Questions

What TV shows make you feel excited?

What TV shows make you feel bored?

What TV character would you like to be?

Interpretive Questions

How does watching TV help you with learning English?

What else do you learn from watching TV?

After watching TV, how are you different?

How has watching TV helped you?

Decisional Questions

What can you do to learn more from TV?

Closing

Thank you. Now we'll go on to our next exercise.

Integrating Learning from an Exercise in an ESL Class

Designed for
Students – Adult

Situation
ESL students are given cards with names and descriptions (i.e., age, gender, job, and hobbies) of people to role-play. They are also given written instructions on how to introduce themselves to each other. The teacher starts by demonstrating how to introduce yourself.
The whole class stands up and mingles. Then they take turns introducing themselves to each other in pairs.

Rational Aim
To practice English language greetings and introductions.

Experiential Aim
To have a fun practice with a minimum of stress.

Hints
Although the exercise is the key teaching tool, the reflection afterwards allows students to consciously integrate what they have learned. The questions need to be easy to understand and to answer.

The Conversation

Opening
Let's find out what we learned in this exercise.

Objective Questions
How many people did you introduce yourself to in the exercise?

Reflective Questions
What part of this was hardest?
What was easiest?

Interpretive Questions
What did you do that was successful?
Where did you have problems? Why?
What did you learn about introducing yourself? About using English?

Decisional Questions
How would you introduce yourself in English now?
Who will introduce themselves to the whole group? Who else?

Closing
I'm glad we all know how to make ourselves known now!

Practicing English while Discussing a Newspaper Article

Designed for
Students – Adult

Situation
An adult ESL (English as a Second Language) class is using a focused conversation to practice new words about traffic, such as stop sign, lane, and intersection. They are discussing a recent traffic accident that they read about in the newspaper.

Rational Aim
To practice new English words about traffic.

Experiential Aim
To gain confidence in speaking English.

Hints
To keep questions simple and to the point, run through the possible answers the students might give before you use the conversation. Adapting the questions to bring out words your group knows will provide more vocabulary practice. Write the questions on the board, so that students can see as well as hear the words. Point to them as you ask them.
When reading the reflective questions from the board, try mimicking anger (shaking your fist), or fear (covering your face with your hands) to give them some ideas.

The Conversation

Opening

First let's read this newspaper article about a traffic accident. Let's talk about this accident for a while.

Objective Questions

What vehicles were in the accident?

What people were in the accident? Drivers? Pedestrians? Others?

What happened in the accident?

Reflective Questions

Imagine what one of the people felt. Make a face to show that emotion.

Interpretive Questions

What caused the accident?

Why did the accident happen?

What traffic accidents have you seen? What happened and why?

Decisional Questions

What is one thing we could do to improve traffic safety?

Closing

Good work!

Reflecting on a Day in a Learning Lab Experience

Designed for
Staff Members

Situation
A group of teachers are at the end of the third day of a ten-day learning lab experience. They have spent much of the day actively creating wall posters and teaching images, transforming the environment of their training room into a vibrant learning environment.

Rational Aim
To summarize the learning of the day.

Experiential Aim
To be excited and pleased with the experience so far, and anticipate the next day.

Hints
Keep the questions specific to the situation, as these are, so the reflection is tightly focused. Tailor the questions for your situation.

Other Applications
You could use similar questions on a worksheet for a solitary reflection on the day's experience.

The Conversation

Opening

We are in the third day of this ten-day laboratory. We've created an amazing environment through our activities today.

Objective Questions

What catches your eye about the Main Hall?

What activities do you remember?

What colors?

What words?

Reflective Questions

What was confusing or overwhelming today?

What was exciting?

Interpretive Questions

What thought or idea or concept became clearer?

What is the key message of this day for you?

Decisional Questions

What have you decided to use from the workshop?

How could you apply what you have learned in your work with students?

Debriefing the Day as a Team

Designed for
Staff Members

Situation
A group of teachers is participating in a learning lab experience as a team. They have taught a class together on this Friday, and are reflecting on the day's learnings and planning the next week.

Rational Aim
To review the significant events of the day and to plan for the next week.
To foster shared learning and reflective practice.

Experiential Aim
To generate team enthusiasm about working together and improving teaching practice.

Hints
Tailor the interpretive questions to the specific happenings of the day.

Other Applications
Weekly team meetings.

The Conversation

Opening

Imagine you are watching a video of this day. Visualize what occurred today, from the time the bus delivered our students until a moment ago when the last student left.

Objective Questions

As we reflect on the day, what is one activity that stands out?

What's one thing we each did today?

Which students participated today who didn't participate yesterday?

When did one of us effectively support the work of another teacher?

Reflective Questions

What surprised you about today?

Where or when did students seem to have difficulty?

Which activities fostered high student involvement and interaction?

At what point were each of us fully engaged in what was happening?

When did you feel best about the contribution you made?

Interpretive Questions

When students had difficulty, what could we have done differently?

Which powerful learning principles did we best achieve today?

What understanding is emerging about where we most need to focus to improve student learning?

How did yesterday's team planning session affect our work today?

What insights do you have about how we can work together better in the classroom?

Decisional Questions

What do we want to contribute to or learn from our colleagues?

Based on what we've seen to date, what can we set as learning objectives for the end of next week?

Who is going to do what on Monday?

What do we need to work on now to prepare for next week?

Closing

Part of what it means to be a "learning team" is to work together, then reflect together on our experience and plan the future.

Celebrating Learnings from a Tough Year

Designed for
Staff Members

Situation
A rural high school has had a rough year, with much tension between groups of staff. An outside facilitator leads the staff in a reflection on the year, to bring the year to closure and allow for planning for the future.
The facilitator draws a large horizontal timeline on the blackboard with the months marked on it, leaving room both above and below the line for cards and writing.

Rational Aim
To create a timeline and story of the journey of the group. To understand what has brought the group to this point.

Experiential Aim
To affirm the whole past, with its highs and lows, successes, and setbacks.

Hints
You can do several streams below the timeline — for example, world events and events in the field of education, with the biggest space for local events.
Another conversation may follow that focuses on insights for the future.

The Conversation

Opening

Let's look at the year we've just had. As we do this, bear in mind that everyone has a different perspective on the year. We do not have to agree on everything, just to listen for the wisdom in what people are saying. We will get out several different answers to each question.

Objective Questions

What events, accomplishments, and setbacks have happened this school year?

Please write them with markers on cards or large sticky notes, and put them on the wall below the timeline in the approximate time period.

Reflective Questions

What were high points for you during the year? (*Make a mark by the event like a tick or an asterisk*)

What were low points? (*Mark differently, by each event.*)

What have you been grateful to someone else for during this year?

Interpretive Questions

As you look at this emerging picture, where would you say there are turning points? (*Mark them as vertical lines above the timeline, dividing it into sections.*)

How would you talk about these turning points – turning from what to what? (*Write the words on both sides of each vertical line.*)

Decisional Questions

How would you name each section of the journey? (*Write the names in each section above the timeline.*)

How would you name the whole year? This has been the year of…?

Closing

This is a powerful journey. You have accomplished many things this year. Sometimes we don't give ourselves credit for what we have done.

Learning from a Historical Scan

Designed for
Staff Members

Situation
A neighbourhood school has just reorganized as a middle school. Many of the teachers live in the neighbourhood but only a few have ever taught at a middle school. Many of the teachers do not know each other. A facilitator has just finished creating an historical scan with the group. On the wall are cards on a timeline with events from education in the province, the school's community, the school itself, and personal events from the teachers' lives.

Rational Aim
To understand implications for the future from a picture of the school and its relationships.

Experiential Aim
To respect each other, and to commit ourselves to the future of the school and the community.

The Conversation

Opening

Now that we have all this data on the wall so we can see it, let's figuratively step back from it and see what we can learn from it.

Objective Questions

What words or events catch your attention in the data on the wall?

What visual patterns catch your attention?

Reflective Questions

What does the data on this wall remind you of?

Interpretive Questions

What story would you tell about what you see on the wall?

Where does our new school fit into this picture?

What factors and principles are guiding the way we operate? What relationships are there between the community and the school?

What do you see happening in the future for this school?

What do you see happening for education in general in the next five years?

Decisional Questions

Which piece of that future are you personally most committed to making happen?

Closing

Thank you. It has been a pleasure to work with you. There is so much commitment to making this school a productive place of learning for the students of our community.

Mentoring a New Teacher

Designed for
Staff Members

Situation
An experienced teacher is mentoring a new teacher to sharpen her teaching skills. The new teacher has just taught a science lesson, after which both teachers sit down to reflect on the experience.

Rational Aim
To have the new teacher establish what was successful and what would be beneficial to try next time.

Experiential Aim
To have the new teacher feel validated in her efforts to teach science.

The Conversation

Opening

I want to help you reflect on today's science class and come up with a couple of strategies to implement in your next science class.

Objective Questions

What do you remember from the lesson? What did you do? Run through the steps.

What was said?

What did students actually do?

What did students accomplish?

Reflective Questions

What was a high point for you?

What excited you? What went well?

What was difficult or frustrating for you?

What strategies would you keep?

What would you change?

Interpretive Questions

What content can you take from this lesson to apply to future lessons?

What teaching approaches can you take from this lesson to apply to future lessons?

What is a key insight you had?

What would you change if you could teach this lesson over again?

Decisional Questions

What strategies will you follow up on?

What techniques or strategies will you focus on for future lessons?

Closing

I've heard your responses to the last questions.

Good work! It is a pleasure to work with you.

Introducing an Unpracticed Skill

Designed for
Staff Members

Situation
A group of teachers in a school are embarking on a new style of working together — mentoring. Some are excited, and others are resistant. Everyone is somewhat apprehensive of the implications of changing the way they're used to working. This initial conversation will introduce other activities.

Rational Aim
To link the skill of mentoring to their past experience in the profession.

Experiential Aim
To enable the group to relate positively to the challenge inherent in learning to be good mentors and to be mentored.

The Conversation

Opening

Today we're going to launch into a relatively long-term project that involves a set of skills we all have some experience with. However, not all our experiences have been the same. Let's talk about it a little.

Objective Questions

As you think about mentoring, what images jump to mind?

From reading or movies etc, where have you see mentoring going on?

What has been an experience you have had with mentoring or being mentored?

What are some things you know about mentoring?

Reflective Questions

What feelings do you associate with mentoring?

What aspects do you expect to enjoy about mentoring?

What do you think you will not like about mentoring?

Interpretive questions

Why is mentoring important?

How will it affect you? Your work?

How might we approach mentoring to make it most effective and helpful for all of us?

Decisional Questions

How can we help each other learn about mentoring — today and over the next months?

Closing

As we've listened to each other's insights, we've already taken the first steps to better understanding mentoring.

Exploring the Topic of a Paper

Designed for
Staff Members

Situation
At their in-service day, twenty staff members of a new middle school are exploring the concept of restitution, a reality-therapy-based technique for helping people become self-directed, self-disciplined, and self-healing. They have read a paper and are ready to discuss its implications. The intent of the conversation is more focused on building respect within the team than it is on actually implementing the concepts.

Rational Aim
To understand the concept of restitution and its implications for the school.

Experiential Aim
To hear and respect each other's opinions.
To begin to be a team.

Hints
The first decisional question in this case is a summarizing question, because the intent of this conversation is under-standing, not action. To take the conversation to action, substitute a question like "What are our next steps in implementing this in our school?"

Other Applications
This conversation can be used with any paper or document.

The Conversation

Opening

Let's explore the implications of this paper on restitution together, in order to hear all the perspectives we have on it. We are not yet ready to act on this, but we need a foundation of understanding to decide what we will do.

Objective Questions

What ideas about restitution does this paper cover?

Others? Any we have missed?

Reflective Questions

What leaves you confused?

Which ones intrigue or excite you?

Interpretive Questions

What more do you need to know?

What are the strengths of the concept of restitution?

What are its weaknesses?

How would applying this concept benefit our school?

What might not work so well?

Decisional Questions

How would you summarize our discussion so far?

What can we do to experiment with applying these concepts in our school?

Closing

It's great to have a chance to hear our different opinions. Let's experiment with the possibilities of this concept, and report back to each other later.

Learning from the Movie *Stand and Deliver*

Designed for
Staff Members

Situation
High school teachers are attending an in-service on image-based instruction methods. They have just watched the movie *Stand and Deliver* written by Ramon Menendez and Tom Musca, from Warner Brothers.

Rational Aim
To focus attention on student needs and motivational techniques.
To initiate a discussion about diverse teaching styles.

Experiential Aim
To experience the presence and influence of a master teacher.
To believe miracles are possible when teachers care.
To inspire the teacher participants to do miracles in their classrooms.

Hints
Expected time: 20 to 30 minutes. Allow time for as many scenes to be named as possible at the objective level, so that the group has the whole movie to work from as the conversation goes deeper.

The Conversation

Opening

This is a very powerful movie. Let's take a few minutes to explore our learnings from it.

Objective Questions

Name the characters in the movie.

Where did the story take place?

What scenes do you remember?

What was the name of the school?

What lines of dialogue do you recall?

What objects did you notice in the film?

Reflective Questions

Where did you laugh?

Where did you witness people's fear?

When did you feel afraid?

Where did you see frustration or get frustrated?

Where did you see hope?

Where did you find yourself in the story?

With whom did you first identify?

Where did you see symbols in the movie? What did they seem to be pointing to?

Interpretive Questions

What were the students up against?

What was the teacher up against?

Where did you see student motivation shift? From what? To what?

What message or messages did the teacher use to accomplish this?

How were they delivered?

Now let's talk about style.

How would you describe the teacher's style?

What was the most outrageous thing he did to allow and encourage learning?

What was the most effective?

(continued)

Learning from the Movie *Stand and Deliver (continued)*

Who are colleagues or teachers you've known as a student who have distinctive styles? How would you describe each of these styles?

How do these differing styles affect student learning?

What are the implications of differing teaching styles for school transformation or reform?

Decisional Questions

What is *Stand and Deliver* about?

What would you name this movie?

Who should see this movie?

Closing

Thank you. I have learned a tremendous amount from this conversation, and I hope you have too.

Processing a Presentation of New Information

Designed for
Staff Members

Situation
Following a training workshop, a teacher has shared her learnings in a presentation about a new communication tool with her colleagues. She is now leading a conversation to help them process their learning.

Rational Aim
To understand the new tool.

Experiential Aim
To feel intrigued with the possibilities of a new communication tool.

Hints
It is very difficult to lead a conversation on a presentation you have just made, because the participants tend to think you are still trying to get a point across, not asking for their real answers. A way around this is to write the questions on the board or flipchart, or stand at the opposite end of the room when asking the questions, so that your change in role is physically visible.

The Conversation

Opening

Let's reflect on this presentation for a few minutes, to think about new learnings and possible applications for us.

Objective Questions

What information stood out for you in the presentation?

What are the key features of this process?

Reflective Questions

At what point did you feel a positive personal response?

What part of the process particularly appeals to you?

What part does not appeal to you?

What parts are you skeptical about?

Interpretive Questions

What might be the impact of this process on our students?

How might this process support you in your work and life outside of school?

What might be the greatest challenge to you in applying this process?

Decisional Questions

When will you use this process?

How will you prepare?

Debriefing Presentations of "Approaches that Work"

Designed for
Staff Members

Situation
A team of teachers from each of several cities across the country is participating in an educational conference. Each team has prepared a report on an innovative approach they are using. Each team reports to the whole group. After each report, each team reflects separately on the presentation they just heard. Each team chooses one person to lead the city team in the following conversation, one person to take notes about questions and reflections for their city team for later work, and one person to keep track of time.

Rational Aim
To share innovative projects and approaches, and begin to look at their possible implications.

Experiential Aim
To appreciate each other's creativity.
To be inspired to be creative in one's own school as a team.

Hints
Repeat the five questions after each team report. Ten minutes for each conversation should be adequate. The note taker can print responses on sticky notes and stick them on a flipchart to allow changes and additions as the group works.
Consider rotating roles of conversation leader, timekeeper and note taker

The Conversation

Opening
Let's talk about the reports we've heard.

Objective Questions
What stood out for you as you listened to what was going on in that situation?

Reflective Questions
Where were you excited about what they were doing?
Where were you unsure or uneasy?

Interpretive Questions
What seems most "on target" about what they are doing there in relation to your school's needs and objectives?
How might this affect us?

Decisional Questions
What are things we should consider for your schools?
What are other things that come to your mind that we should consider?

Closing
Reflection as a total group on the day.

Debriefing a Role-Play on Team Teaching

Designed for
Staff Members

Situation
A half-day in-service session on team teaching is provided for all the teachers in an alternative school. They want to decide its usefulness in their school. The session starts with a role-play of two teaching teams, one whose members share common goals and one with diverse members with various goals and approaches.

Rational Aim
To understand how both teams with common goals and with strongly diverse goals can work together effectively.

Experiential Aim
To experience the challenges of teamwork.

Hints
Write out the role-play in advance, giving enough direction so that it can be done easily.

The Conversation

Opening

Let's explore the possible learnings behind these two role-plays.

Objective Questions

What did you hear the teachers say or tell each other in each role-play?

How did the teachers look at each other?

What body language did you notice on each team?

Reflective Questions

What part of the role-play made you most uncomfortable?

What looked like the most fun?

What does team teaching feel like?

What did it look like to you in these role-plays?

Where have you seen similar situations in real life?

Interpretive Questions

What are the strengths and weaknesses of the team with common goals?

What were the strengths and weaknesses of the team with strongly diverse goals?

How do students benefit from team teaching?

What do you think constitutes effective team teaching?

What are the benefits of team teaching that make it worth the effort?

What are some of the arguments against team teaching?

How did today's demonstration respond to these arguments?

Decisional Questions

What have you learned about working in teams?

How might we use team teaching in our school?

Closing

Our learnings and recommendations from this conversation will help us decide how to use team teaching in our school.

Understanding Society from a Teenager's Point of View

Designed for
Staff Members

Situation
In a high school staff meeting at the beginning of the year, the principal is working to build a respectful, collaborative environment of teachers, administrators, and students.

Rational Aim
To see society as teenagers see it.

Experiential Aim
To give credence to teens' lived experience.
To prevent burnout of teachers.

Hints
It is easy to slip out of the imagined role while doing this conversation, especially at the interpretive level. The facilitator should gently bring people back to the perspective. You may also try having each person imagine seeing through the eyes of more than one teenager, for a richer experience.

The Conversation

Opening

Think of a teenager you know or have encountered recently. Imagine that you are that teenager, looking out from their eyes. Spend a little time looking at the world around you through their eyes.

Objective Questions

As you walk, ride, or watch TV, what are some of your observations about society?

What do you see, hear, smell, taste, or feel?

Reflective Questions

What were your feelings as you made your observations?

Who seems to like you as a teenager? Dislike you? What do they say to you?

Interpretive Questions

Still as a teen, how do you feel teens are projected in our society?

What is a value that comes from your observations and reflections?

What would you say to those you like? Those who dislike you?

Which elements of the society you are encountering should be retained? Changed?

Decisional Questions

What role do you wish to play in this society?

What impact do you believe you can make as a teen to improve society?

As you say good-by to these teenagers and come back into yourself, what will you take into the future?

Understanding Learning Styles

Designed for
Parents and Community

Situation
Parents and teachers in a multicultural community are exploring learning styles together, in order to make sure that the school is providing opportunities for students of all cultures to learn effectively.

Rational Aim
To deepen the understanding of one's own learning patterns and learning patterns of others.

Experiential Aim
To gain strength and confidence in one's self and one's own learning styles, as well as an appreciation of others and what can be learned from them.

Hints
As the facilitator, it is appropriate to check on each small group, but it is wise not to interrupt or interfere unnecessarily. The small groups may need more time than allotted to share their experiences. After the small group work, you may want to have a conversation with the larger group such as the one on page 97.

Other Applications
Any topic where people have previous personal experience that will be useful to bring out new learning, for example, teamwork.

The Conversation

Opening

First let's go around the table and introduce ourselves to the whole group.

Learning doesn't just happen in school in traditional ways of teaching. I remember that when I was a little girl, I learned how to make cookies from my grandmother. She didn't tell me anything. She just made the cookies, and I helped her. When we got to the part where you roll the dough out so you can cut it, she put her hands on mine and guided them. I still enjoy making those cookies.

We are going to break into small groups to discuss how we learn best. These are the questions I would like you to answer, in this order *(hand out papers)*. In this discussion, there are no wrong answers. Each person has a piece of the puzzle, and they are all different. If we really listen to each other, we will all be wiser at the end.

Objective Questions

(Go around the group) What are some events or times when you really learned something or you observed real learning taking place, either inside or outside school? Or when you learned an old or traditional skill?

What did you learn in this situation?

Who or what was the "teacher" if there was one?

Reflective Questions

What parts of these experiences sound like the most fun?

What parts sound difficult, painful, or boring?

Interpretive Questions

How did you learn in this situation?

What actually helped you to learn?

What are common elements in our stories of successful learning? For example, was it quiet or noisy? Were you moving or still? Were you alone or with others?

Were there visual images? Words? Sounds? Other factors?

What were some unique elements?

(continued)

Understanding Learning Styles *(continued)*

What do these common elements tell us about what factors are important for our best learning?

Decisional Questions

How would we summarize the factors that make learning successful for us as a group?

Closing

How will we report back to the large group our common elements and factors for successful learning?

Integrating Reports from Small Group Work

Designed for
Parents and Community

Situation
Parents and teachers have discussed their experiences of successful learning in small groups, and have summarized their findings to report back. Each group reports succinctly without interruption. After all the reports, they hold the following conversation.

Rational Aim
To agree on a list of patterns of learning.

Experiential Aim
To experience an "Aha! We have powerful ways of learning that the schools can respect!"

Hints
In this conversation, all the reports are given before the reflection, in order to hear the whole picture first. Sometimes it may be helpful to ask for questions of clarification after each report, then do the rest of the conversation at the end.

Other Applications
Any plenary session where groups are reporting back.

The Conversation

Opening
Let's pull together our learnings as a large group.

Objective Questions
What words caught your attention as you heard these reports?

Reflective Questions
What came as a bit of a surprise or was unexpected?

What made you laugh?

Where did you think, "Oh yeah, I understand that!"

What images came to mind?

Interpretive Questions
What threads did you hear running through the reports?

Which of these was said the most often?

Let's draw all this together — What combination of elements make for successful learning?

Decisional Questions
What might this all mean for providing culturally appropriate learning in our school?

How do we implement our learnings?

Envisioning the Future of Education

Designed for
Parents and Community

Situation
Parents, teachers, staff and students have come together to plan the year. They start with a conversation to set the largest possible context for themselves to sustain their action.

Rational Aim
To imagine the role of education in the 21st century.

Experiential Aim
To experience the possibilities for education in the future.

Hints
The objective and reflective level questions in this conversation are drawn from the imagination, making this conversation very different from many others in this book.
It is important to take enough time in the opening to stand firmly in 2010 before a conversation. Locating one's self in a different time is hard to hold if you have not had some practice at it, and if you don't hold it, you find yourself inserting your present beliefs into the future.

The Conversation

Opening

Close your eyes for a moment. Imagine you stumble into a time machine, which starts up. When it stops, you discover you are in the same place, but in the year 2010. Look around you at all the things you see going on in 2010.

Objective Questions

Standing in the year 2010, what were some key events of the past decade for business and industry? Government? Social groups and communities? Education? Your region?

Reflective Questions

Assuming that education has made a significant contribution to society, what does it mean now in 2010 to be educated?

How is education organized in 2010?

How are responsibilities distributed?

Point to one profound learning over the past decade, since 2000.

What has been learned about education between 2000 and 2010?

Interpretive Questions

Now, coming back into this time and space, what would you need to know to live effectively in the 21st century?

Decisional Questions

What needs to be done today in order for this picture of the 21st century to be realized?

What are you willing to commit to?

CHAPTER 7

Making Communication Effective in Groups

The conversations in this chapter focus on facilitating clear communication in groups. They are designed to build shared understanding and respect, and to help bring a group to wiser decisions.

For students, these conversations provide tools for working cooperatively.

For principals and staff, they allow thoughtful dialogue in a tight time frame for staff meetings and planning sessions.

For parent and community councils, they can guide effective and respectful discussion of issues from many perspectives.

Introducing a Cooperative Learning Project

Designed for
Students

Situation
A sixth grade class is studying world geography. Students have been assigned to do team projects in groups of four. Each team has an assignment sheet with the outcomes expected and the process they are expected to use to produce them. One student facilitates a conversation for the group to understand the assignment.

Rational Aim
To enable students to have a focus for their assignment and a plan for getting it done.

Experiential Aim
To develop interest and commitment to the assignment.

Hints
Rewrite this conversation using appropriate language your students will use. Give all the students the questions.

Other Applications
Use the same conversation for every project to teach the pattern of analyzing a group problem. Students may also use this individually to prepare for a project.

The Conversation

Opening

OK, here is what the teacher has given us.

Objective Questions

What things does the assignment sheet say we have to do?

What does it say the final result should look like?

What parts don't you understand? Can anybody explain, or should we ask the teacher?

Reflective Questions

Which part of this assignment looks most interesting to you?

Which part looks boring or uninteresting?

Which parts are you really good at?

Which part looks like an interesting challenge?

Which looks like it may be hard work, or a lot of work but interesting?

Interpretive Questions

What will this look like when we're done? *(Brainstorm)*

Let's draw a picture or a chart of what we want it to look like (we can always change it).

Decisional Questions

What are all the things we have to do to get this done? Let's write them on sticky notes.

Who should do them? Let's write names by the actions.

When will we do each of these? Let's put them all on a calendar.

What's our first step and who will do it?

When do we check back?

Closing

Let's get going!

Conferencing during a Group Project to Evaluate and Plan Action

Designed for
Students

Situation
A group of junior high students is working on a month-long social science project. The teacher takes 15 minutes to conference with each group to make sure they are progressing in a helpful direction.

Rational Aim
To establish a one-week action plan for a group in progress.

Experiential Aim
To strengthen confidence and trust among group members and with the teacher.

Hints
Despite reassurances, students are often afraid to admit difficulties in front of teachers. If you sense there is more difficulty than they are admitting, you may have to ask them to repeat the discussion on their own after you leave them. If that is the case, they need the questions written out on a sheet – maybe a form for them to fill in.

Other Applications
This conversation can work for any project, including staff projects.

The Conversation

Opening

I want to talk with you for a few minutes to make sure your project is coming along well. I will not be grading you on your answers to my questions, so do be honest, please. If you are having difficulty, it will be important to say so, because there is plenty of time to straighten things out, but it will only work if we raise our questions and resolve them.

Objective Questions

What did you do on this project last week? Show me your notes, activities, actions, etc.

What were the results? Show or demonstrate them quickly.

Reflective Questions

What were you really happy about in what you did?

When did you feel frustrated?

What was the group's high point? Low point?

Interpretive Questions

What have you learned about the topic?

What have you learned about working together on this topic?

Decisional Questions

What changes do you need to make?

What action do you need to take to proceed with the project?

Who will do these things?

When will you do them?

What do we need to arrange in order to be successful?

Closing

Good work! We'll check again next week.

Thinking about Leadership with Students

Designed for
Students

Situation
A middle school includes a personal development curriculum for students during the homeroom period each day. Today's topic is leadership.

Rational Aim
To discover qualities of leadership in the students' own experience

Experiential Aim
To choose to develop their own leadership capacity

Hints
This is a conversation designed to be held with students, but a dry run with teachers beforehand will also be useful for the teachers' own reflection.

The Conversation

Opening

Let's go around the room — Who is someone in history or literature (or a movie) whom you consider to be a leader, for example, from arts, politics, business, community affairs, organizations, education, science, social justice?

Who are a few living people you can think of that you see as leaders?

Who are some people you know that you consider as leaders?

Objective Questions

What characteristics of a leader do you observe in these people we just named?

What are or were some of the responsibilities of these leaders?

Reflective Questions

What is exciting about being a leader?

What is frightening about being a leader?

Interpretive Questions

What are some common qualities of leadership in the people we've named?

Which are unique characteristics of some of these leaders?

Which of these do you consider to be leadership qualities?

If someone were to become a leader, what qualities would they need to develop?

Which of these qualities seem really important to you?

Decisional Questions

What are some things you can do to cultivate these qualities in yourself? In others?

Closing

Everyone in this room has the capacity to be a leader in some positive way, if we choose.

Solving a Problem with a Group Technology Project

Designed for
Students

Situation
Grade eleven and twelve technology students are in the midst of building a robot for a national contest. Two weeks before the contest, they put the robot through a test, and it tips over every time it goes up the ramp. The students have to solve the problem on their own, and quickly.

Rational Aim
To develop a solution to the problem and an action plan to do it.

Experiential Aim
To create team commitment to dealing with the problem.

Hints
Teaching students a generic form of this process for solving problems will provide them with life long problem solving skills.

The Conversation

Opening

Okay, we'll have to put our heads together to solve this one.

Objective Questions

What did you notice just before the problem started?

Which direction did the robot fall?

What other things did you notice — hear or see?

What have we tried to solve the problem so far? What happened?

Reflective Questions

What similar situations have you seen?

What else do we know about this kind of problem?

Interpretive Questions

What are some possible reasons this is happening? Explain your ideas.

What might be an underlying cause?

What are some things we could do to deal with this?

Decisional Questions

What shall we do first?

Who will do it?

Closing

Let's go!

Creating an Anti-Racism Policy

Designed for
Students

Situation
A racist incident erupted last week in a high school. The immediate situation was resolved, but students want to create a school policy to guard against its recurrence. A diverse group of students meets after school.

Rational Aim
To develop the elements of an anti-racism policy.

Experiential Aim
To build students' confidence that they can handle future situations.

The Conversation

Opening

We don't want anything to happen again like last week's incident. Let's create the elements of a policy that can guard against racist behavior in our school. Let's start by reflecting on what went on last week.

Objective Questions

What are some facts and observations you actually saw or heard with your own eyes and ears last week? Let's try to put together a multi-dimensional picture.

Reflective Questions

What made you angriest?

What frightened you most?

What struck you as absurd or inappropriate?

Interpretive Questions

What were some of the reasons this happened?

What is underneath these reasons?

What policies or structures in the school may allow or cause this to happen?

What changes would help prevent racist behavior here?

Decisional Questions

What elements of policy should we recommend?

Which ones shall we include in the draft?

What will we do next?

Who will do it?

Closing

When a draft is written, let's all get back and review it.

Responding to a Draft Policy

Designed for
Teachers and Staff Members

Situation
A union representative for teachers has been given a draft policy on vacation time from the school board. She wants some feedback from union members in order to present a considered response back to the board. She has asked a small group of teachers to meet after school to talk about the draft policy.

Rational Aim
To have well-considered alternatives to a draft policy statement to be included in a response to the draft statement.

Experiential Aim
To have front-line staff experience themselves as co-creators of a policy that affects them.

Hints
The material could be distributed ahead of time if it would not ignite political maneuvering. Silent reading time in the meeting is usually a good idea, even if participants have had it in advance. Consider having the group read the statement out loud, with one person reading each paragraph.

The Conversation

Opening

I want to submit a response to this policy draft from the school board about vacation time. I want your feedback to draft my response, so that we present a well-considered alternative. Could you give me some help? Please look at this policy for a moment.

Objective Questions

What phrases did you notice in the draft policy?

What are the key points?

What is the stated rationale behind this proposal?

Reflective Questions

How do you anticipate the draft policy will or might affect you?

How might this policy be helpful?

How might it be unhelpful?

Interpretive Questions

What changes are represented by this draft policy?

How does it differ from past policies?

How does the draft fit with the collective agreements — similarities? Differences?

What will be the impact on staff?

What are some alternatives to these proposals?

Suppose we were to suggest some changes. What are some suggestions for how we might helpfully change this?

Decisional Questions

What are we saying no to?

What do we say yes to?

What items do we support?

How shall we organize our response?

To whom shall we submit the response?

Closing

Thank you. I'll draft a response with our insights and run it past you before I submit it.

Implementing Recommendations for Change

Designed for
Teachers and Staff Members

Situation
A school is concerned with new legislation requiring teachers to integrate special needs students into regular classrooms.

Rational Aim
To understand the recommendations and develop an initial plan to deal with them.

Experiential Aim
To ensure teachers feel their concerns have been heard. To generate hope that they can continue to resolve these issues.

Hints
This conversation is designed from the assumption that the "recommendations" must be implemented. To adapt it for an initial exploration of the meaning of recommendations, add more questions at the interpetive level. To create a more detailed implementation plan, add more detailed questions at the decisional level.

You might need to write out the questions on a flipchart in the opening and ask people to hold answers until they are raised. People with strong concerns, who are not used to a structured conversation, often want to get right to the reflective level so they can vent frustration. Laying out an agenda gives people a way to park their thoughts and see a larger picture.

The closing of this conversation is a brief conversation on the experience of the larger conversation.

The Conversation

Opening

Let's do quick review of the report to look at the objective data. We need to understand the recommendations so we can decide what to do with them.

Objective Questions

What are the specific recommendations in this report?

What particular people or resources does it call for?

What points do you need clarity on?

Reflective Questions

What is your first reaction?

What images do you associate with these recommendations?

Interpretive Questions

What differences will these recommendations make if they are implemented?

What would be the advantages? Disadvantages? Which will have the most impact? The least impact?

What changes will be required for us?

Decisional Questions

What do we need to do with these recommendations?

What is our first step?

Who will do it?

Closing

This conversation has certainly put us in a new place.

What were the high points and low points of today's conversation?

What have you learned?

How would you describe this experience?

Evaluating Staff Surveys and Recommendations

Designed for
Teachers and Staff Members

Situation
The School Growth team has surveyed all staff members about a curriculum event for junior students. The results of the surveys have been summarized by a couple of people, and the recommendations listed.

Rational Aim
To explore recommendations from staff and identify the best ones for future curriculum events.

Experiential Aim
To commit to make needed changes.

Hints
This conversation can be used to reflect on any survey results.

The Conversation

Opening

The School Growth team needs to review the results of the staff survey about the curriculum events held for junior students in December.

Read survey summary aloud, perhaps sharing the reading roles.

Objective Questions

What words or phrases catch your attention?

List the recommendations made from the survey.

Reflective Questions

What are your reactions to these words, phrases or recommendations?

What surprises you?

Interpretive Questions

Which of the recommendations are most important for you? Why?

Which needs to be dealt with first? Why?

Decisional Questions

What do we need to do to implement these recommendations?

What is our next step?

Who will do it?

Closing

These are important decisions and will help us make a difference in future curriculum events.

Gathering Ideas from a Focus Group on a Web Site

Designed for
Teachers and Staff Members

Situation
A focus group of teachers is meeting to gather requirements for creating a web site.

Rational Aim
To set the context for a workshop getting input from teachers and administrators into the creation of a web site for area teachers.

Experiential Aim
To build anticipation for use of the site.

Hints
Personal reflection on a larger topic related to the particular decision at hand often encourages creative and practical thinking. In this case, understanding the experience of finding useful information can help increase the usability of the web site content and design.
This conversation can easily be followed by an implementation workshop. The decisional level question is the workshop focus question.

The Conversation

Opening

The topic today is to gather requirements for our new web site, which will be a resource for information for teachers in our area and beyond. Let's start by introducing ourselves around the table. Please give your name, your school, and one thing you enjoy about teaching. Because the web site will be a resource for information, I would like us to think about the larger context of searching for information first, then focus on our web site.

Objective Questions

Think back over your life and share one experience that you've had searching for information.

What are some of the quests for information you have gone on as teachers?

In what ways have you used the web as a resource in searching for information for your teaching?

Reflective Questions

Using a metaphor, what were those searches like? For example, I was searching for (x) on the web the other day and it felt like being in a house with a hundred rooms and each room had about 5 doors. There were so many options to choose from.

Describe a successful experience. *(Just a couple of responses)*

Describe a less than successful experience. *(Just a couple of responses)*

What was it like when you found the information you were looking for?

What was it like when you hit brick walls or dead ends?

Interpretive Questions

What were the keys to finding the information you were after? What else helped you?

How do you anticipate a web site will serve teachers?

What is the importance of having an area teacher web site?

How will it affect you personally? Your work?

(continued)

Gathering Ideas from a Focus Group on a Web Site *(continued)*

Decisional Questions

What resources do you especially want to see on a web site for our teachers?

What should the web site look like?

What would you include?

What would you put on the front page?

Closing

With this input, our local teacher web site should be much more useful to teachers.

Improving Staff Meetings

Designed for
Teachers and Staff Members

Situation
Primary and Junior Division faculty members in an elementary school have met regularly to plan together for a few years. There is some anxiety that the meetings need to be more time-effective due to increased pressure on the school day. The division head decides to reflect on the meeting structure with the group.

Rational Aim
To provide direction for how to improve the structure of future staff meetings.

Experiential Aim
To allow the staff to gain ownership of and commitment toward their own meetings.

Hints
Since the decisional level answers are the key ones in this conversation, it may be helpful to write the answers to this level on the board or a flipchart one by one in order to get a clear consensus. Write the name or names of people taking responsibility beside the action. Document the results for the group.

The Conversation

Opening

Let's look back at how these meetings have been structured over the past couple of years.

Objective Questions

What are some things we have done in our meetings over the last couple years?

How have we organized our meetings? Not "how well", but how have we structured them?

What topics and concerns were addressed?

Reflective Questions

What seemed to be working well?

What has been frustrating for you?

Interpretive Questions

What needs have emerged?

What has been the impact of these meetings in your classroom? In your school?

How have the meetings fit in with your school plan?

What is the most significant thing about these meetings?

What trends are emerging in our discussion so far?

Decisional Questions

What do you suggest we continue to do?

What do you think needs to be stopped?

What changes are needed?

Let's summarize what we have said about the changes we need in our meetings?

Who will take responsibility for any of these changes?

Closing

This should make a big difference. The next meeting should be much more effective. At the end of the year we will do this again to see how we're doing. Thank you.

Making a Mission Statement Meaningful

Designed for
Teachers and Staff Members

Situation
A newly merged school board has created a new mission statement. Each school staff member has been asked to look at this mission statement and work to make it real in the local school.

Rational Aim
To understand the underlying meaning of the mission statement.

Experiential Aim
To own the mission statement and be a part of the team it belongs to.

Hints
The interpretive questions will get boring if they do not go really fast. It is asking the same question over and over. Treat it as one question with a few follow-through ones that are only used if necessary.

Other Applications
This conversation can be used to discuss values, principles, or vision as well.

The Conversation

Opening

Have the mission statement written and visible to all participants — on a flipchart, board or overhead projector.

Let's discuss this and see what meaning we can draw out of it.

Objective Questions

Would volunteers from the group each read a section from the mission statement?

What words or phrases stand out for you?

Reflective Questions

What visual images are triggered or pictures come to your mind as you see and hear this read?

What part of this is really exciting? Scary? Demanding? Right on target? Confusing?

What word or phrase of this strikes you as the most powerful?

Interpretive Questions

What do these statements of our mission look like in real life, in our day-to-day operations?

How do these statements affect our work?

How do we play them out in day to day activities?

When you see these being acted out, what do you see?

What does this tell us about who we are as an organization, as educators, or as a group?

Decisional Questions

What implications does this have for our actions in the future?

Which part or parts of this are you personally most committed to?

Closing

This mission statement has taken on new life for me, and I hope for all of us.

Planning Curriculum

Designed for
Teachers and Staff Members

Situation
There is a new curriculum guideline out for Social Science. It describes expectations and has some lesson suggestions, but does not designate exactly how to do the curriculum. All of the teachers affected by the guideline are meeting to plan together how to implement the curriculum. They will do common lesson plans to ensure all students in the school have the same opportunities, and so that teachers can share resources.

Rational Aim
A comprehensive curriculum plan ready for lesson plans.

Experiential Aim
Experience the strength of teamwork

Hints
At the objective level, putting the curriculum sections and key concepts on a graphic on the wall will be very important for continued reference throughout the conversation. Cards, each with a separate idea, will be useful, as they can be moved around to group and sequence the topics.

The Conversation

Opening

We've got two hours to discuss the social science guidelines and flesh out what they mean for our curriculum plan.

Let's make sure we understand what is asked for here.

Objective Questions

As you flip though this, what are the sections of this curriculum?

Looking at this curriculum section by section, what are the key concepts in each section?

Reflective Questions

What images come to your mind as you read this?

What would be fun to teach?

What makes you uncomfortable?

Interpretive Questions

What are the enduring understandings that we want students to come away with?

What are some ways we can organize these concepts to teach them effectively?

How shall we group and sequence the topics?

What blocks of time do we need to accomplish these objectives?

At what times during the school year?

What materials will we need?

What materials can we use?

Decisional Questions

Who will do the lesson plans for each time block?

What is our next step?

Closing

Thank you, everybody, for your insight. I'm so glad we have such different gifts and perspectives. The students are going to really benefit from this curriculum.

Improving Parent-Teacher Interview Evenings

Designed for
Teachers and Staff Members

Situation
Teachers in a large city high school have expressed concerns about parent-teacher interview evenings. At a staff meeting, the principal takes time to listen to teachers and facilitate the creation of a solution to the problems.

Rational Aim
To understand the issues involved in the parent-teacher interview evenings.
To develop a plan for the remaining meetings scheduled for this year.

Experiential Aim
To struggle with the conflicting interests of all involved in parent-teacher interviews.
To feel ownership of the plan developed.

The Conversation

Opening

This conversation will help us decide about the format of parent-teacher interviews. We have recently experienced two parent-teacher interview evenings. Think back to those two evenings.

Objective Questions

What words or phrases come to mind to describe what you saw and heard at the last interviews?

What caught your attention?

What types of parents were there?

Reflective Questions

What was your first response to these evenings?

What excited you?

What frustrated you about them?

Interpretive Questions

What concerns do you have about parent-teacher interviews?

What are some of the root issues behind our concerns?

What are the implications of these issues for our school?

Which of these are the most important? Why?

Which of these issues must be dealt with first? Why?

Decisional Questions

What actions or ways of organizing the evening would make them more helpful or effective?

What changes do we need to make?

What are some of the things we can do to solve the problems?

Closing

Let me try to sum up. We agree that . . . . (Re-state the decision).

Identifying Issues as Input to a Collaborative Plan

Designed for
Teachers and Staff Members

Situation
The business roundtable of the Chamber of Commerce and an educational foundation want to find ways to assist new charter schools to build on effective business practices and become financially viable. Roundtable members plan to hold a conversation with the leadership of each school. The results will be used to plan a joint retreat to plan how to improve the schools' management.

Rational Aim
To identify underlying financial and management issues of the school.
To have some suggestions for the content of the retreat.

Experiential Aim
To experience having wisdom and input into what is needed. To experience support and morale-building from external advisors.

Hints
It would be wise to write the answers to the objective question on a flip chart or blackboard to provide a visual, external reference point. This process can use a consensus workshop at the interpretive level to identify underlying issues. See the appendix and bibliography for a description of this method.

The Conversation

Opening

The purpose of this conversation is to get an idea of what business practices you can use help with to improve your school's management.

Let's begin with introductions: What is your name, position, and something you appreciate about this school? Let's start our conversation by sharing a bit about your concerns.

Objective Questions

What are some of the specific financial and management arenas you spend your time on?

Reflective Questions

Which ones demand the most time?

Which ones are the most complex?

Which ones are very closely related?

Which seem to be going well?

Which are giving you difficulty?

Interpretive Questions

Considering all these different arenas, what specific answers do you have to this question: What are the financial or management issues we need to solve in order to thrive?

Which of these point to similar underlying issues?

How would you name these underlying issues?

Which ones, if "solved", would make the greatest difference for us?

Decisional Questions

Looking at these, what implications do you see?

Where might collaboration with the business community and with other charter schools help?

Which issues could you take on yourselves?

Closing

Once our group meets with all the schools, our plan is to come together for a management retreat. Which would you prefer: to spend one day to clarify one issue or to spend two days creating a solid plan to deal with all of these issues?

Understanding a Policy and Resource Guide

Designed for
Teachers and Staff Members

Situation
A resource person has been asked to provide information and guidelines on school-based decision-making (SBDM) to about thirty school leaders.

Rational Aim
To know the major elements of provincial SBDM policy and the relationship between the Resource Guide and SBDM policy.

Experiential Aim
To have a sense of the importance of SBDM in each work situation.

Hints
This is a brief conversation. It is designed to enable a group to gain an overall image of material quickly. Deeper conversation can take place after this quick overview discussion. This kind of conversation can be used to replace or enhance a presentation. This kind of conversation can be used with a large group if the questions through the interpretive level are discussed in conversations around small groups, then shared with the whole group. This requires careful planning of time to allow the small groups to work, yet share periodically with the large group for wider insights.

Other Applications
This conversation can be rewritten to fit other new policies or written initiatives.

The Conversation

Opening

Welcome. Let's go around the table and introduce ourselves: give your name and one question you have about SBDM.

Here are some resources. The package of materials contains the provincial SBDM policy and key parts of the *Resource Guide*, including the table of contents and the question and answer section.

Objective Questions

What are the major requirements spelled out in the written policy?

Skimming the *Resource Guide* table of contents, what topics catch your attention?

As you skim the question and answer section, what catches your attention?

Reflective Questions

What parts do you find most interesting?

Which parts intrigue you?

Interpretive Questions

What information here do you find helpful to know?

What links do you see between the policy elements and the *Resource Guide*?

What are ways you might use this information in your work?

What is one new idea you have from looking at this material?

How does it relate to your role in the school, jurisdiction or school council?

Decisional Questions

How might you use the *Resource Guide* in your role?

If you had two minutes to explain SBDM policy to someone else who was not in this session, what would you say?

Closing

What additional information do you need to know about SBDM as a result of this session?

Sharing a Quarterly Team Progress Report

Designed for
Teachers and Staff Members

Situation
A dispersed, district-wide special project team has quarterly progress report meetings.

Rational Aim
To have clarity on progress since last meeting.
To have appropriate plans for future action.

Experiential Aim
To deal with anxieties and build team confidence.

Hints
You can use a pre-printed report form designed according to the conversation method to enable participants' reflection. Before the meeting, each person fills out a "simple team report" form and brings it to the meeting (see the report form in Chapter 10).
Get brief, bullet-point answers from each person. Move quickly. Be sure everyone participates. Appoint a reporter.

The Conversation

Opening

To begin this meeting, let's share what has happened this quarter. First we'll go around the group and get one answer from each team member, and then we'll open it up for additional comments from anybody.

Objective Questions

What has happened since the last time we met? Think of accomplishments, events, and activities related to our task.

How many people have been involved?

Reflective Questions

What is going well in your work?

What struggles or difficulties have you encountered?

Interpretive Questions

Looking to the future, what are one or two chief challenges we face in continuing to work on this project?

Decisional Questions

What actions do you suggest to deal with our challenges?

What are key actions we intend to take?

Who will be responsible for each?

Closing

I think we should do something to celebrate our progress and our future. Let's have a treat and toast the future.

Reflecting on a Writing Team's Work

Designed for
Teachers and Staff Members

Situation
A group has worked hard to revise the teacher evaluation guide. Afterwards they reflect on their work together and the product they have created, in order to decide how best to use it.

Rational Aim
To identify ways to introduce and implement the use of the revised guide.

Experiential Aim
To experience their work affirmed.

The Conversation

Opening

Let's review the work we've done and figure out where to go from here.

Objective Questions

If you were a newspaper reporter, how would you describe the steps we went through today — first, second, etc.?

Reflective Questions

What about our work do you feel best about?

Where did we struggle the most?

Interpretive Questions

How will the product, with our proposed revisions, compare to the previous one?

What are its strengths?

What weaknesses can you see?

How will it be used?

How will it make a difference?

Decisional Questions

What can be done to ensure the revised guide is used effectively?

What are the next steps?

Closing

Thank you for your effort!

Talking through Roles and Responsibilities

Designed for
Teachers and Staff Members

Situation
Experienced and beginning teachers in a school district have spent an in-service day planning projects together in mentor and protégé pairs. The program coordinator is leading a conversation with the whole group at the end of the day.

Rational Aim
To gain new images of the tasks and responsibilities associated with the roles of mentor and protégé.

Experiential Aim
To inspire protégés and mentors with the important and challenging work ahead.

The Conversation

Opening

Now that you have planned your next projects, let's talk a bit to compare insights between teams.

Objective Questions

What did you plan today?

What scenes, phrases or events stand out for you?

From your work today, what are some of the major tasks of the mentor in your project? What are some major tasks of the protégé?

Reflective Questions

What are you excited about doing?

What part of the work ahead seems like a heavy burden?

Interpretive Questions

In a sentence, what would be a job description for your project for the protégé? For the mentor?

If I were to ask you about the importance of the work you will do on your project as a mentor, what would you say? As a protégé?

What have you learned about working in this way?

Decisional Questions

What is the first action you have planned in your project?

When is the date of your first meeting?

What other support will assist you to successful completion of the project?

Closing

Your work together is going to make a big difference for our students' learning. Thank you very much.

Determining Staff Development Needs

Designed for
Teachers and Staff Members

Situation
A principal needs to work with staff members to determine their in-service needs.

Rational Aim
To gather recommendations for in-service training events

Experiential Aim
To create anticipation and motivation for in-service training events.

The Conversation

Opening

One of my tasks this week is to arrange our in-service schedule, and I wanted to make sure I understand what you need.

Objective Questions

What are some of the program issues or changes that concern you? I will write these on the board.

What other needs have you noted in the area of program? Curriculum? I'll write them on the board as well.

What points do you need clarified regarding these issues?

Reflective Questions

Which items seem like they'll be easiest to deal with?

Which items present the greatest challenges?

What is already in place that could help you to deal with these issues?

Interpretive Questions

Are any of these issues similar or connected in any way?

What are some of the possible teaching strategies to use in dealing with these issues?

What experience do staff members have in dealing with these issues?

What do you think would be the best approach to address some of these concerns?

Which of these is best addressed in an in-service session?

Decisional Questions

Which of these teaching strategies is the most immediate need?

How can it be addressed in an in-service training session?

Who needs to be involved?

Where would be a good place to start?

What other help might you need?

What else can we do to assist you?

Closing

This has not only given us an in-service program, but it has given us other ways to address our development needs. It is a pleasure to work with you! I'll get back to you with the schedule as it works out.

Assessing Need for Staff Development in a School Visit

Designed for
Teachers and Staff Members

Situation
A program support person from the school board office is visiting principals to determine staff development needs. She conducts this focused conversation in a half-hour meeting with each principal, taking notes as the principal talks.

Rational Aim
To gather prioritized needs for staff development.
To know what support is needed from the board.

Experiential Aim
To enable the principal to feel supported and heard.
To take responsibility for dealing with needs.

Hints
In a one-on-one conversation, these questions may have to be asked more informally. Pick and choose the appropriate ones for each level.

The Conversation

Opening

I want to take a few minutes with you to get your thinking on staff development needs in your school this year, so we can plan how to support you.

Objective Questions

What are some of the program concerns that your staff members have expressed?

What other needs have you noted?

Reflective Questions

Which items strike you as easiest to deal with?

Which items present the greatest challenges?

What is already in place that could help you to deal with these issues?

What other questions do you have about these issues?

Interpretive Questions

Are any of these issues connected in any way?

What are some of the possible strategies for dealing with these issues?

Which staff members have experience in dealing with similar issues?

What do you think would be the best approach to take in addressing some of these concerns?

What resources do you need to assist you in dealing with these concerns?

Decisional Questions

What is the most immediate need to deal with?

Who needs to be involved?

How will you start?

How can I best help your school's needs for staff development?

Closing

Thank you for your time. We will use your input and that of other principals to focus our staff development programs.

Deciding What Course Material to Purchase for a Language Program

Designed for
Teachers and Staff Members

Situation
An elementary school has made a priority focus on literacy over the next few years. Although resources are limited, they have decided to spend some money on upgrading their reading and language resource materials. At a staff meeting, the resource teacher is leading staff in a discussion of what to buy.

Rational Aim
To establish criteria for purchasing resource materials, and to decide on next steps.

Experiential Aim
To experience responsibility as a group for making a difficult decision.

Other Applications
Not only can you use this conversation for other curriculum material decisions, but also for making other difficult financial decisions, with some adaptation.

The Conversation

Opening

As you know, we have a priority this year on better reading skills. This is just the beginning of improving literacy resources in the school.

Objective Questions

What materials are you presently using in your classroom?

What other resources are available in the school?

What other resources do you know about that we don't have?

Reflective Questions

What do you like about our current resources?

What do you dislike about them?

What other materials would be helpful?

Interpretive Questions

How effective have our current materials been?

How have they been helpful?

What impresses you about those you like?

What student needs are not being met in this area?

What does this tell us about what we are missing and what we need?

What are the basic criteria we need to use in evaluating potential resources?

If we have limited funds, what would be your priorities?

Decisional Questions

Are there any specific materials these values suggest?

What do we recommend we acquire with our limited budget?

What should we do next?

Closing

I think we have some good direction for us to move toward increasing our reading resources in an effective manner. Thank you for your time.

Identifying Educational Trends

Designed for
Teachers and Staff Members

Situation
A large conference of educators tries small group conversations as an inspiring way to start a plenary session on the future of education. People are sitting at round tables of eight to ten people.

Rational Aim
To identify trends in education.
To wrestle with the future of education.

Experiential Aim
To sense that they are responsible for the future of education.

The Conversation

Opening

Let's take a little time to have small group conversations about trends in education.

Each table has a sheet of questions. Choose a facilitator and answer the questions in order, so that we have a shared experience as a whole group. At the end each table will be asked to share a few insights, so you will also want to have someone take notes on the conversation.

Objective Questions

Let's go around the table. Give your name and your role in education in the past five years.

What are some trends, innovations, or new directions in education that you have seen or experienced recently?

Reflective Questions

Where have you been excited about the trends in education?

What worries you about some of the trends?

Interpretive Questions

How have your images of teaching shifted in the last ten years?

What are your images of education for this century?

What do you want to see in the future?

What major concerns do you have when you think about education?

Decisional Questions

What can we do to encourage the positive trends and discourage the negative trends?

What does the future of education depend on?

Closing

Each group is asked to share an insight or two with the whole group.

Inspiring Effective Teaching

Designed for
Teachers and Staff Members

Situation
Before the school year begins, the principal of an elementary school brings his staff together to inspire them to think about teaching students in a holistic way.

Rational Aim
To articulate the qualities of an effective human being in today's world.

Experiential Aim
To inspire participants about effective teaching.

Hints
Taking the time to reflect on inspiring topics can re-energize people and make their work more effective.

The Conversation

Opening

As we teach, we are models to our students whether we like it or not. Let's take a few minutes to think about some people who were models for us.

Objective Questions

Let's go around the table, and each person name a teacher you will never forget.

What did you learn from that teacher?

How did you learn it?

Reflective Questions

Now, go beyond the usual category of teachers. Who are the people you think back to (or dialogue with) when you need help or inspiration?

What do you find yourself copying or learning from these people?

Interpretive Questions

What are some of the elements of their success?

What is it that enables them to be effective?

What did they do to develop these qualities?

Decisional Questions

What can we do to increase our own effectiveness?

What can we do to develop the effectiveness of our students as human beings?

Closing

We want to keep this in mind as we prepare our students to be effective human beings.

Planning Staff Development for
Working with School Community Councils

Designed for
Teachers and Staff Members

Situation
Teachers in a school have been given a document on implementing school community advisory councils. Some teachers are concerned about the changes required of them, as parents become more active. The principal decides to have a conversation with staff as an item on the staff meeting agenda, about what professional development would be useful to ease the implementation.

Rational Aim
To explore the document on school community councils. To provide some input about professional development to the implementing team.

Experiential Aim
To experience some feeling of interdependence.
To feel valued.

The Conversation

Opening

The purpose of this conversation is to provide input to the Board about professional development to work with school community councils. Let's focus on the document for a few minutes to be sure we understand it.

Objective Questions

What are the section headings for this document?

What does the document say is the mandate of school community councils?

What does the document say the membership should be?

What does it say about the group's start-up, and the duration in office?

What does it say are the functions of other parent groups?

Reflective Questions

What excites you about the opportunity to get involved?

What frightens you?

What skills do you already possess that will facilitate implementation?

What is your past experience with our school's parent groups?

Interpretive Questions

What words in the document need further clarification?

In what parts of this program will there be a need for professional development?

What skills do you need to develop?

How would they best be developed?

With whom should they be developed?

Decisional Questions

What recommendations do you have about topics for professional development?

What do we need further training on?

When should training take place?

Who will help take these recommendations forward?

Closing

We will make sure that the implementing team has the results of this conversation. Thank you.

Reflecting on Effective Learning
at a Principals' Conference

Designed for
Principals

Situation
A new superintendent in a city school district has called a meeting of principals. This meeting represents a significant shift in agenda and format for these principals. They are accustomed to sitting and listening to the superintendent transmit information with little time for questions and answers and no time for discussion and dialogue. As a result, this is the first opportunity for many of the principals to talk and get acquainted. Prior to the conversation, the principals are engaged in an icebreaker to set the stage for the conversation.

Rational Aim
To get to know other principals in a more informal setting than usual. To engage in a dialogue about "learning" with their peers. To identify groups based on areas of interest in education for future dialogue.

Experiential Aim
To value the time spent in dialogue and making new connections. To begin to trust their new superintendent.

Hints
For a group larger than 20 or 25 people, the first three levels of conversation could be done in small groups, then shared with the group before the decisional questions.

Other Applications
This conversation leads to small groups that can continue to work on their decisions. This conversation can be useful for any other topic where the formation of small groups is part of the aim.

The Conversation

Opening

Let's think a little about what enables effective learning. We all have wisdom and that would be helpful to others.

Objective Questions

What contributes to learning in your school? What specific examples can you share from your experience?

What are some different factors you have observed that no one has mentioned yet?

Reflective Questions

What is it about learning that you are most passionate?

What intrigues you about learning?

What are the greatest challenges to real learning that you see around you?

Interpretive Questions

Which of these elements of learning are the most important?

Which of these elements of learning have the most impact for the learners in your school?

What do you do, as a principal, which contributes to these elements of learning?

Decisional Questions

What is it about learning that you want to focus on?

What areas of interest related to learning would you like to continue to dialogue about? (*Write the list on a flip chart.*)

Which areas would you like to sign up to do more work on?

If those people who have signed up for a particular area form a small group, we can continue to dialogue in small groups.

Who will help convene the group for each area of interest?

Closing

We will continue our dialogue in a similar fashion throughout the year.

Understanding a Regional Structure and its Benefits

Designed for
Teachers and Staff Members

Situation
Six regional consortia for professional development have been established. The person responsible for the project needs to familiarize all directors and senior managers in the department of education with the concept. Forty people have come to a meeting.

Rational Aim
To become familiar with the purpose of the regional consortia for professional development
To know how the regional consortia might benefit participants in their curriculum work, student evaluations, and implementation of the core goals and values of their departments.

Experiential Aim
To appreciate the practical benefit of the regional consortia.

Hints
If small groups are going to come up with common results, it is important that they all follow the same process. The questions may be written on an overhead or flip chart, or printed and put on each table.
Another short conversation with the whole group on what they've heard from the small groups may pull together the whole group's learnings and create consensus.

The Conversation

Opening

This meeting is to make sure all of you understand the purpose of the regional consortia, and can see how they might benefit your work. Let's talk first in groups of five so that we all have a chance to speak. We will start with this newsletter, which describes the facts of the program. Each group will use the same questions, so that all groups have a similar conversation.

Here is the newsletter and a sheet with the following questions. Take a few minutes to read it.

Objective Questions

Who is involved in each of the regional consortia?

What is their stated purpose?

What is their structure?

Reflective Questions

What worries or challenges come to mind as you imagine this initiative playing out?

What positive potential can you see?

Interpretive Questions

What positive potential can you see?

How can the regional consortia benefit professional development?

How can they affect the parent councils?

How will they improve work in the classroom and the students?

How will they affect your own work?

Decisional Questions

What can we do to contribute to their success?

Closing

Will each small group please share their key insights with the whole group?

Setting the Context for Planning

Designed for
School Board Members

Situation
A school board has set aside a full day to begin preparing goals for the next three years. The board and its senior administrators are having a conversation to prepare for their goal setting exercise.

Rational Aim
To raise awareness about the events and trends which have shaped the school district. To consider the potential of this day to affect the future of the district.

Experiential Aim
To awaken a sense of fascination with the district's eventful history. To evoke optimism among participants grounded in a history of accomplishment.

Hints
If time allows, invite participants to respond to the first question by telling a brief story about their involvement in or knowledge of events described. An individual school that is preparing to develop school goals can use the same conversation.

The Conversation

Opening

We have committed this day to the beginning the process of goal setting for our school district. When we set goals, we are deliberately forecasting the future of our organization.

The responsibility for planning is best carried out by the team that provides leadership to an organization. For a school district, at the heart of that team is the school board and the senior administrators.

As we begin this process, we should be mindful of the rich history of our school district. If we had time, we might cover a wall with a timeline filled with important events, and then reflect on the trends that have made us who we are today. To make the best use of our limited time today, we will instead reflect on our history in a conversation, and consider the implications for the future.

Objective Questions

When was this district founded?

What are some of the key events that you can remember from the history of our school district?

What changes have taken place in our enrollment levels?

When have we made important changes to our programs or facilities?

When did changes in personnel affect us?

When did you personally first become involved with our school district?

Reflective Questions

What do you remember about those times when we have made progress?

Where have we struggled?

What do you associate with those struggles?

Interpretive Questions

If we were to divide our history into chapters, where would you divide the chapters?

What would you call these chapters?

What new vantage point does this discussion give us on our school district's progress?

(continued)

Setting the Context for Planning (continued)

Decisional Questions

What does this conversation tell us about who we are and where we are going?

How has this conversation helped prepare us for our school district's planning exercise?

Closing

Thank you for your memory, wisdom, and insight. This makes me very proud to be a part of this school district, and full of positive anticipation for the future.

Debriefing an Intensive Brainstorming Session

Designed for
Parents and Staff Members

Situation
Seventy-five parents and staff of a School Planning Committee of a province-wide education association are finishing an intense three-hour session, in which they have done workshops in small, self-selected groups on how they can help school councils or committees. At the end they need to do a focused conversation to bring all their experiences together.

Hints
This conversation can be used to debrief any tough session.

The Conversation

Opening

Let's quickly reflect on our experience today.

Objective Questions

What did we hear, see and do this morning? (Two to five word impressions)

Reflective Questions

Where did you laugh?

Where did you feel hopeful?

What parts caused you anxiety or concern?

Interpretive Questions

If you were to do this session over, what would you add?

What would you leave out?

What was the value of this session for you?

Decisional Questions

What is one thing you'll do to follow this up at your school?

Closing

Thank you for your incredible wisdom and commitment.

Making a Mid-Course Correction of an Action Plan

Designed for
Teachers and Parents

Situation
At the beginning of the year, a group of parents and teachers set an ambitious plan to reorganize the classes in the school. It is now January, and the government has imposed new priorities, which demand attention in a different area. People are beginning to question why they should continue reorganization at all.

Rational Aim
To develop a realistic revised action plan to deal with the changes to the situation.
To identify next steps required in order to complete the revised action plan.

Experiential Aim
To relieve guilt and pressure on the group.
To experience renewed commitment to a more appropriate plan.

The Conversation

Opening

We want to see where we are on the implementation of our action plan.

Objective Questions

Look at our original plan. What have we completed already?

What has happened since we started implementing this plan — events, actions, accomplishments, victories?

What do we see as the steps to be completed in our existing plan?

What parts of our plan have not been completed?

What new information do we have regarding the plan?

What events or changes have affected our implementation?

Reflective Questions

What concerns you about the implementation of our plan?

What do you still feel is important?

Interpretive Questions

What parts or elements of this plan need to be completed as we designed them? For example, what still seems to be on track, or are very high priority activities that would not be wise to let go.

Which parts of the plan need to be reconsidered?

What impact does completing this plan have on the new government priorities?

Which parts are most critical to complete?

Given that we are limited in time and resources, now that we have additional priorities, which parts can we reasonably complete?

What new elements do we need to add to our plan?

Decisional Questions

What do we need to include in our revised plan?

What steps can we take to ensure completion of our goal? Set up an outline of what to include.

When will we need another mid-course check?

Closing

Tremendous. Let's get going!

Discussing Implications of New Performance Standards with Staff

Designed for
Teachers and Staff Members

Situation
A school district staff meeting is discussing how to implement the newly mandated performance standards and benchmark exams. The changes are controversial, but there is no choice but to implement them.

Rational Aim
To thoroughly understand the implications of implementing the mandated performance standards and benchmark exams.

Experiential Aim
To develop the commitment to address concerns and to make the changes work

Hints
Notice the smaller series of objective, reflective, and interpretive questions within the objective level. The first question is objective, the second two are reflective, and the last four are interpretive. This sequence ensures that the group has digested the information before going on.
This conversation may be followed later with the one on page 133 with parents.

The Conversation

Opening

Next year our instruction will be modeled around performance standards and benchmark exams. Let's think through ahead of time what the parents' and teachers' possible questions, concerns, objections, and criticisms about this process might be. Then we can answer the questions ourselves. After we have thought through possible objections, we can work with teachers and parents to address them and make the mandate work to the students' benefit.

Let us review for ourselves the features of teaching the performance standards and having benchmark exams, starting with a fact paper describing the changes.

Objective Questions

What words or phrases stand out?

What do you need to have clarified?

What worries you? What pleases you?

What are the main points?

What ideas and innovations could come from teaching this way?

How does it differ from the current method of instruction and evaluation?

What does this method of instruction and evaluation NOT do?

Reflective Questions

As you think of implementing these exams, what makes the hair on your neck rise?

What potential vulnerabilities do you see?

What potential benefits do you see?

Interpretive Questions

Why do you think the Department of Education and the Legislature have decided to require these exams?

What will parents and students be thinking as they see these changes implemented?

What specific questions will they want to ask?

What particular objections can you hear them raising?

(continued)

Discussing Implications of New Performance Standards with Staff (continued)

How can we address these concerns and make this mandate work to the benefit of students?

Decisional Questions

What suggestions do you have for how we might go about it?

What is our next step?

Closing

This conversation can better prepare us and our school district to address the concerns, objections, and obstacles that parents and teachers present when confronted with performance standards and the benchmark exams.

Exploring the Implications of Performance Standards with Families

Designed for
Parents and Community

Situation
The intention is to talk with the community in a major effort of faculty and aides to visit the families and discuss the benchmark tests. Each faculty member will be assigned one or more families, which will make it possible for a contact person to coordinate visits for all the siblings at the school.

Rational Aim
To ensure that families understand the performance standards and the possible impact on their children.
To gather ideas on how to assist students.

Experiential Aim
To build trust between families and the school.
To relieve anxiety about performance standards.

Hints
These two conversations may be followed later with others specific to identified problems.

The Conversation

Opening

Here is an outline of the upcoming changes *(give the handout)*. Take a few minutes to read this. I'll let you look it over, and then we can talk.

Objective Questions

What are the key facts about the recent changes requiring a high school exit exam and benchmark exams?

Reflective Questions

What concerns do you or your family have regarding this new practice?

What do you like about it?

Interpretive Questions

Why do you think the schools and the Department of Education think this is so important?

How might these new tests affect your family?

Decisional Questions

What are some of the things the community and school can do to help in preparing kids for these exams?

Closing

This conversation can better prepare our community to address the concerns, objections or obstacles present when confronted with performance standards and the benchmark exams.

Reflecting on a Year-long Study Group

Designed for
Parents and Teachers

Situation
A study group of parents and teachers has been meeting regularly through the school year. Attendance is beginning to drop off as spring approaches, and they decide to review their reasons for existence.

Rational Aim
To review goals and ideas.

Experiential Aim
To identify common goals and directions and record them.

The Conversation

Opening

Let's review reasons for the group to clarify direction.

Objective Questions

Why did you join the group?

What goals did you have when you joined?

Reflective Questions

How do you feel now about this group?

How do you feel you've grown?

How has the group helped you?

What have been opportunities you've experienced?

What have you enjoyed?

Interpretive Questions

What would you say has been the most worthwhile aspect of this group?

What's been least helpful?

What goals have been met?

What would you like to see happen in future?

What direction do you sense from the group?

Decisional Questions

What do we need to do over next few months?

Who will take on which tasks?

Closing

Who will record our findings for the next meeting?

Assigning Projects to New Facilitators

Designed for
Parents and Community

Situation
A school board committed to community participation has created an ad hoc group of facilitators. A list of projects needing facilitation has already been identified. The projects need to be assigned so work can begin.

Rational Aim
To enable the facilitators to identify their strengths and interest, and choose their projects accordingly.

Experiential Aim
To empower the group to choose their initial projects.

The Conversation

.Opening

Going around the table, let's each introduce ourselves with our name and a bit about our expertise, strengths, and interests.

Objective Questions

Looking at the list of facilitation projects, what projects catch your attention?

Reflective Questions

As you look at the list, which projects excite you?

Which ones frighten you?

Which projects need more attention?

Interpretive Questions

What is it about the projects that worry you?

What makes you more comfortable with certain other projects?

What additional information do you require about any of the projects?

What suggestions do you have to alleviate your fears about these projects?

Decisional Questions

What method could we use to choose our projects?

Using this method, who will do which project?

How can we support each other to make working on these projects a pleasant and productive experience?

Closing

We'll make sure these assignments are written up, and that we schedule a time to meet again as a team to check on our progress.

Gathering Feedback on Proposed Sex Education Curriculum

Designed for
Parents and Community

Situation
A large urban school board has created a new draft curriculum on human sexuality for grades seven to nine. They have consulted with a broad spectrum of passionate interests, but need to get specific feedback from a diverse representation of stakeholders before moving to a final draft. About fifty people have come to an evening meeting. After opening with an overview on the whole process, they have been divided into small groups, one for each theme or subtopic. Facilitators are guiding each small, diverse group. A writing group will take lists of recommendations from this meeting and weave them into the new draft.
Each small group facilitator leads their small group through the following conversation.

Rational Aim
To have a range of recommendations and suggestions for the final draft of the human sexuality curriculum.

Experiential Aim
To experience having been heard.

Hints
For such a hot topic, the facilitators have to be prepared to be both open to a wide diversity of answers, and firm to guard the process. Naming the steps of the process at the beginning can give the group a structure for their participation. (For example, objective:

The Conversation

Opening

Let me outline the process that will be used.

Let's go around with quick introductions — please give your name and what brings you to the table.

These are the pages of the curriculum that are concerned with the theme of this small group. Take a few minutes to look them over. Now let's make sure we all see what is in the curriculum already before we start to respond to it.

Objective Questions

What words or phrases stick out for you?

What are the key points the curriculum makes in each section? We'll go through it section by section.

What questions do you have about what the document means?

Reflective Questions

Where does something in this document trigger an experience you've had?

What parts of the curriculum do you like best?

Which parts are you concerned about?

Interpretive Questions

Why are you concerned about these parts?

What are the implications of this curriculum for students' growth and development?

What values or principles do you see included in this document? Give a concrete example from the document.

Decisional Questions

What recommendations do we want to suggest to the writing team?

What other values or principles would you include in the curriculum?

What other information would you add to the curriculum?

What other changes would you suggest?

What resources would you add to the bibliography?

Anything we've left out?

(continued)

Gathering Feedback on Proposed Sex Education Curriculum *(continued)*

data, getting clear on the document itself; reflective: initial reactions; interpretive: getting out the underlying significance and implications; decisional: making recommendations.) Setting out participation guidelines will allow the facilitator to return to them to keep people on track. You may want to restate working assumptions and clarify the facilitators' roles (i.e., the facilitator has no opinions while they are facilitating, we use a process to make sure that the whole group gets to its objective, etc.).

The facilitator may also need to restate the theme and the product (rational aim) of the small group work.

Participants may want to argue with each other's views. The facilitator needs to get all the perspectives out without allowing arguing. This conversation does not assume that the group comes to agreement on recommendations, only that they are discussed thoroughly and listed. Recommendations in this case can include more than one perspective or opinion. If pulling together one statement is difficult for the group to agree on, skip this step and take several recommendations forward.

We will give this whole list to the writing team.

If we can do this quickly, it may be helpful to give them some priorities from our perspective.

From our list of recommendations, which would we say are most important?

What have you heard us saying the most strongly as a group?

Closing

The writing team will take our recommendations and those of the rest of the groups, and will use them to refine the curriculum. Let's go back to the large group.

Establishing A Parent Advisory Council

Designed for
Parents and Community

Situation
The Education Department for all schools has mandated parent or community advisory councils (PACs). The principal has invited some active parents to think about how they can organize a successful council.

Rational Aim
To establish a strong supportive parent advisory council with at least a twenty-member turnout for monthly meetings.

Experiential Aim
To have willing, committed participants and volunteers in school life and activities.

The Conversation

Opening

Let's look at this article on "How to Organize Successful Parent Advisory Committees". Take a little time to look the article over.

Objective Questions

What do you see in this paper that catches your attention?

What key words or phrases jump out at you?

What does the paper say about why parents get involved in PAC's?

What does it say about why parents don't get involved?

Reflective Questions

What past memories, experiences or feelings do you have with advisory groups?

What positive experiences have you had? Negative experiences?

What angers or excites parents about working with schools?

What do parents worry about?

What opportunities do parents see?

Interpretive Questions

What would a strong PAC do?

What results would we want from it?

How can we increase the awareness of parents and community?

What are the benefits of a strong PAC to parents? To students? To the school? To the community?

Why is it important to develop a strong PAC?

How can we increase awareness of parents & community in the PAC?

How do we make PAC membership a priority to parents?

Decisional Questions

What are our first steps in forming a PAC?

Who is going to do what?

Closing

Let's check back with each other in a week's time to see how we're doing.

Establishing a Community Advisory Council

Designed for
Parents and Community

Situation
A school has decided to establish a Community Advisory Council (CAC). A small group of parents and staff is exploring how to get it started.

Rational Aim
To explore the benefits of having a Community Advisory Council.
To develop an action plan to establish a Council.

Experiential Aim
To generate excitement and trust.

Hints
Although this conversation is on a similar topic as the one about starting a parent advisory council, it starts with a different concrete beginning point. You can compare the two conversations to see how a different starting point affects the discussion.

The Conversation

Objective Questions

How would you describe the characteristics of our school?

How is it unique?

What are its gifts?

How are community members participating in the school?

Reflective Questions

What is motivating about being involved?

What frustrations need to be identified?

What has been working well with the current community involvement?

Interpretive Questions

Why do people choose to become involved?

Where do you see a CAC fitting into the system?

What would it do?

What issues could it help with?

What do you see as the role of the CAC...in the community? ...in the school?

How might our school change because of this?

How might the CAC be organized?

Decisional Questions

What do we need to do to get started?

Who will do these things?

Closing

I'm glad we're finally on the road to getting this done. Thank you, everyone, for your time and creativity.

Editing a School Pamphlet

Designed for
Parents and Community

Situation
The School-Community Council needs to revise the school profile pamphlet that is given to students every year.

Rational Aim
To identify key areas of the profile that need to be updated.
To make a decision about what changes to make.

Experiential Aim
To be excited about making changes and contributing ideas to the school profile.

The Conversation

Opening

As you are aware, one of our tasks of the School Community Council is to produce a school profile—a pamphlet telling about our school. Here is our profile from last year *(hand out profiles).*

Objective Questions

As you look at the pamphlet, what are the major sections?

How would you describe the general layout of the pamphlet?

As you read through the pamphlet what are some main words or phrases that get your attention?

Reflective Questions

How does the layout strike you?

What part really grabs your attention?

Which part doesn't hold your attention?

Interpretive Questions

Who are we really trying to reach?

How will it be used?

What does the profile presently communicate to you?

What else does it need to communicate?

What shifts in our situation need to be communicated?

What new information do we want to get across?

What changes might accomplish this?

What changes are most important? Why?

Decisional Questions

What have you heard our members say are the key areas to deal with first?

What is our next step in making these changes?

Closing

This is an important step. Thank you for your help.

Increasing Participation of Businesses in a School-Community Council

Designed for
Parents and Community

Situation
Lots of parents and social agency people are involved in the School-Community Council (SCC), but few business people are involved. The Council is concerned and puts a discussion on the next meeting agenda.

Rational Aim
To make recommendations and decide about how best to get businesses involved in the School-Community Council.

Experiential Aim
To act on best recommendations and make decisions about business involvement for future meetings of the Council.

The Conversation

Opening

A concern arose in our last meeting about the lack of community business involvement for our School-Community Council.

Objective Questions

How many businesses are there in our community?

What other types of business do we have?

Reflective Questions

What is intriguing about the possible involvement of these businesses?

What is a bit scary about their potential involvement?

Interpretive Questions

What are the benefits of their involvement to us? To them?

What are the dangers?

What are other implications of business being involved?

Why do we think businesses are not involved at this time with the SCC?

Decisional Questions

What are some things we can do to get businesses involved?

What is our first step?

Closing

These are important decisions and will have an impact on our future as the School-Community Council.

Unblocking Poor Parent Involvement

Designed for
Parents and Community

Situation
The Parent Advisory Council is in despair because fewer and fewer parents come to every meeting. A small group is taking on more and more essential functions. The council is faltering.

Rational Aim
To create options for increasing involvement.

Experiential Aim
To encourage parents to stay involved.

Hints
The objective data is hard to get here, because parents who are not showing up may not have spoken to anyone. It is important to actually find people and ask their opinions, or you will only be operating out of interpretations from other people. To achieve breakthrough, you need objective data to solve the problems that really exist. Before this conversation takes place, you may need to have people call other parents who have come in the past and no longer participate to ask them the questions, and then add them to the group's answers.

The Conversation

Opening

We want to focus on what we should do to get parents interested in the Parent Advisory Council for the school. Let us review what has brought us to this point.

Objective Questions

What background data do we have? How long has the organization been operating?

How many members do we have? What is the membership potential?

How many parents showed up for our biggest meeting? The smallest?

What were the topics discussed in these meetings?

How have we invited people to meetings? How do parents find out about the meetings?

What comments have you heard from parents about these meetings?

Reflective Questions

What draws parents to the meetings?

What activities have generated the most involvement?

What invitation strategies have worked most effectively?

What parts of involvement in the PAC are really energizing?

What is the most frustrating part of involvement in the advisory council for you? For other parents?

Interpretive Questions

What are we looking for in the area of parent involvement?

What factors prevent us from generating the kind of parent involvement we want?

What can we do to involve more parents?

Decisional Questions

Which change shall we pursue first?

Who will do it?

Closing

We'll begin as soon as possible to implement these.

Reflecting on a Survey

Designed for
Parents and Community

Situation
A parent council has distributed a survey on school safety. The results have been tabulated, and they are considering the results at a parent council meeting.

Rational Aim
To make decisions about priority needs, based on the survey.
To explore options for actions to address identified priorities.

Experiential Aim
To develop trust in each other and the commitment to work together for change based on common concerns.

The Conversation

Opening

Here are the actual survey results. Take a moment to skim through them.

Objective Questions

What results here catch your attention?

What points of this report do you need more information on?

Reflective Questions

When you heard the results, what experiences came to your mind?

Which survey comments sound most familiar?

Which are unexpected or surprising?

Interpretive Questions

What are the key issues or concerns raised?

Which of these items is the most important? Why?

Decisional Questions

What are some things that we can do to deal with these issues?

Which of these actions are the most important?

What are our next steps?

Who will do them?

Closing

Thank you. Let's go to our next agenda item.

Focusing the Purpose of a Parenting Workshop

Designed for
Parents and Community

Situation
A group of parents has come to a workshop on positive parenting. The facilitator wants to set the purpose and the agenda in a participatory way.

Rational Aim
To focus the group's expectations.

Experiential Aim
To have the group experience its creativity and wisdom.

The Conversation

Objective Questions

Let's go around the room, giving your name, and one thing you would like to gain from this workshop on positive parenting.

Are there any other things you would like to work on?

Reflective Questions

What excites you about the positive parenting idea?

What worries you about this topic?

Interpretive Questions

What have you heard the group name as some common goals we have for this workshop?

Which of these common goals would you make a high priority?

Decisional Questions

Which of these goals are you personally committed to?

What are our next steps?

Closing

Your thoughts have helped me choose which elements to focus on in this course. Let's move into our first exercise.

CHAPTER 8

Preventing and Solving Problems

The conversations in this chapter are designed for dealing with conflicts between students, between staff and parents, or staff and staff. Some help resolve misunderstandings on hot issues before conflicts occur. Others help solve thorny problems.

All of these conversations acknowledge deeply felt emotion, and move through it to thought-out solutions.

Talking through Misbehaviour with Preschool Children

Designed for
Students

Students
Talking through misbehavior with preschool children

Situation
This morning a mother had a real fight with her preschoolers on their way to school. She wants to talk it through with them, since they were all upset and they don't want it to happen again.

Rational Aim
To identify an area of difficulty in cooperating.
To begin to think about ways of solving this difficulty.

Experiential Aim
To resolve to change their behavior.

The Conversation

Opening
We need to talk about what happened this morning.

Objective Questions
What things happened before we went to the school this morning?

Reflective Questions
What did mommy's face look like this morning? Make a face like that.
What did your face look like? Make a face like that.

Interpretive Questions
What made mommy mad?
What made you mad?
Why do you think this happened?

Decisional Questions
What should we do differently tomorrow?

Closing
I'm really glad we can solve problems like this so we don't have to have them again.
(Big hug.)

Conversation after a Playground Fight

Designed for
Students

Situation
Certain students have been trained to intervene in peer conflicts on the playground. A fight has just happened and an older student is handling the situation.

Rational Aim
To understand what caused the fight and have a plan for solving future problems.

Experiential Aim
To experience that the situational problem is resolved. To be confident about handling similar situations in the future.

Hints
Of course, you will have to substitute the real behavior that students report in their answers to the objective questions in the reflective questions.

The Conversation

Opening
Let's see if we can work this out.

Objective Questions
Stacey, tell me in your view what happened?
Brenda, now you tell me what happened.

Reflective Questions
How did you feel when she called you names?
How do you think she felt when you hit her?

Interpretive Questions
Why do you think this happened?
What are some of the reasons for both of your actions?

Decisional Questions
What can you do differently if this happens again?
What can we do now to get back to what we were doing before this problem?

Closing
All right. Let's try to have some fun.

Increasing Understanding of Sexual Harassment

Designed for
Students

Situation
A high school counsellor is meeting with small groups of students to talk through social issues and how to deal with them.

Rational Aim
To bring each participant to an understanding of sexual harassment.

Experiential Aim
To be able to recognize and act when seeing sexual harassment.

Hints
The second conversation in the closing is a good one to process the experience of the main conversation, when it has been long or difficult. It can be left out if the main conversation is short.

The Conversation

Opening
First let me read a definition of sexual harassment.

Objective Questions
What is sexual harassment in your own words?
What actually happens in a situation of sexual harassment?
What are some examples you've seen either in real life or on TV?

Reflective Questions
Put yourself in someone else's shoes for a moment. What worries you the most about sexual harassment?
What images do you associate with a situation of sexual harassment?

Interpretive Questions
What are some effects of sexual harassment?
What are some values in our society that foster sexual harassment?

Decisional Questions
What can we do if we see sexual harassment happening?
What can we do to prevent harassment from happening?

Closing
Let's reflect on our experience of this conversation. What words did you hear?
What was interesting or frustrating?
How are we different as a group because of this session?
What did we learn?
How will this change your behavior in situations of sexual harassment?

Improving Behavior on the School Bus

Designed for
Students

Situation
A bus driver has stormed into the principal's office with a complaint about rowdy behavior on her bus that is endangering her driving. The principal has all the kids on the bus sit down together for a conversation.

Rational Objective
To enable students to understand the consequences of their behavior.

Experiential Aim
To develop the capacity to consciously choose behavior. To be encouraged to monitor their own behavior responsibly.

The Conversation

Opening
We need to talk about the behavior on the bus.

Objective Questions
What have you seen kids do on the school bus?
What has the driver asked you not to do?
What have you done?

Reflective Questions
What is one thing that someone has done on the bus that makes you mad?
What is something you've done that made somebody else mad?
What actions upset the driver?

Interpretive Questions
How does this bus behavior affect other students?
How does it affect the way the bus driver drives?
Why is this a problem?

Decisional Questions
What choices can you make about your behavior on the bus?
What can you do differently?
What choices will you make?

Closing
We will talk again next week and see how things are going. I'm looking to see how much better you can make this.

Understanding Bullying

Designed for
Students

Situation
Students, staff members and parents in an elementary school are exploring the phenomenon of bullying.

Rational Aim
To understand bullying behavior, and its effects.
To begin to identify options for dealing with bullying in the school situation.

Experiential Aim
To share students' perspective on bullying in the school.
To be committed to work together to build a trusting and safe environment.

Hints
Be very careful to focus on the behavior and not label individuals or groups. The people, themselves, are not the problem. They may well have problems, but labeling people as bullies or victims will exacerbate the problem rather than solve it.
In a conversation that includes children and adults, be prepared to ask questions in more than one way so that everyone understands the question and can participate.

The Conversation

Opening
Today we are going to have a conversation about bullying.
Let's start with some working assumptions: everyone has wisdom and important ideas to share; there are no wrong answers; everyone hears others and is heard.
We'll start with a definition of bullying from the dictionary.

Objective Questions
What words or phrases caught your attention as I read this definition?
Think of a bullying situation you have observed. Think of the overt, direct, clear situations, but also think of the subtle ones as well—take about a minute to think.
What do you see? What actually happened?
What do you hear?
What do you physically feel, touch?
Describe the people involved.
Where and when does it happen?

Reflective Questions
Where or when have you seen or experienced something like any of these situations?
How did you feel?
What was frustrating for you?
How did the people around react?

Interpretive Questions
What are the common threads in these experiences?
What are the characteristics of those who use bullying behavior?
What are the characteristics of those who are the recipients of this behavior?
What have you learned?
Why do people behave in this way?
What are different ways this behavior can be dealt with?

Decisional Questions
What changes are needed?
What can we do to deal with this behavior in our school?
What are you committed to do?

Closing
We will share the changes and commitments we have mentioned to other parents and staff. Your commitments to making changes are extremely valuable to your school. Thank you for your insight.

Solving a Conflict between Students

Designed for
Students

Situation
The teacher has just broken up an escalating argument in her classroom. She wants to solve not just the current argument, but the pattern of conflict.

Rational Aim
To resolve the conflict between the two students.

Experiential Aim
To develop the ability to talk through conflict.

Hints
At the interpretive level, the answers may lead to other specific questions that cannot be anticipated. Follow the conversation, adding questions that probe a little deeper into the underlying issues, until it is time to move to the decisional level. Language will need to be made specific for each situation and age level.

The Conversation

Opening
We are going to work out this problem together, so that we all feel comfortable. If we can't, I'll make the decision as to the consequences of your behavior.

Objective Questions
(Addressing each person, one at a time)
Tell me, what is it you did?
What did you say? Just use "I" statements.

Reflective Questions
(To each person)
What were you feeling when this happened?
Did you have any other reactions?

Interpretive Questions
Let's get to the bottom of this.
(To each person)
What do you think she meant by that?
Why do you think that?
What are you discovering about why this happened?

Decisional Questions
What can each of you do to clear this up (or resolve it)
What do we need to make sure this doesn't happen again?

Closing
Let's go back to work.

Understanding Rude and Bullying Behavior

Designed for
Students

Situation
Parents and the teacher of a grade four to six classroom are concerned about rude and bullying behavior between the students. One of the parents volunteers to facilitate the discussion.

Rational Aim
To understand what some of the reasons were for the behaviors.
To get suggestions for what might be done about the issues from everyone.

Experiential Aim
To enable parents and students to hear one another's views.

Hints
It is difficult in a potentially volatile factionalized situation to have a parent from one of the factions facilitate. It will help to explain to everyone what the process is and why you are doing it this way (before and during the meeting). It is helpful to set some ground rules because of the intimidating aspect of having a whole lot of parents present. It helps if some of the more confident kids speak up and have the support of their parents.

The Conversation

Opening
We're going to talk for a while to see if we can sort out some problems that have been happening in the past few weeks. I'm going to focus the discussion by asking some questions in a carefully planned order.
Some ground rules:
Everyone's idea is important.
We are not looking to blame anyone.
So let's get started.

Objective Questions
What are some of the things that are happening right now (both good and bad)? Let's get an answer from each person.

Reflective Questions
What part of what's going on are you happy about?
What upsets you?
What worries you?

Interpretive Questions
Why are you worried?
What are some of the reasons things are not going well?

Decisional Questions
What can we do about these issues?

Closing
I would like you to turn to the person next to you before you leave and thank them for their participation. And thank you to all of you.

Discussing Peer Pressure with Students

Designed for
Students

Situation
Seventh grade teachers in a junior high school decide to have conversations on social issues with students in their homeroom classes. The first conversation is on peer pressure.

Rational Aim
To recognize the power peer pressure can have on an individual.

Experiential Aim
To recognize the power students have inside them to resist peer pressure.
To understand their own exertion of peer pressure on others.

Hints
You might give out the main objective questions all at once, give an example and let the group tell their stories as distinct units. They answer any or all of the questions. You will need to decide about questions and clarifications, because seventh graders will want details when friendships are involved. This could be long, but good.

The Conversation

Opening
Let's talk about how friends and other students influence your decisions or actions.
Think about a time when you were with a group of friends and had to make a decision.

Objective Questions
What was the situation?
What were the choices?
Where and when did it happen?
Who was involved (no names needed)?
What was said?
What happened?
What was the decision?
What are similar experiences others have shared with you (no names needed)?
When have you done something under the influence of others?
What is a situation in which you have exerted pressure on a friend?

Reflective Questions
How do you feel when someone or a group is trying to get you to do something?
How have you reacted when you felt pressured?
How do you think your pressure makes others feel and react?
What part of dealing with peer pressure is hardest? What is easiest?

Interpretive Questions
Why do you think this pressure or influence is being exerted?
What are some of the benefits that may result from pressure?
What are the dangers?
How do you deal with pressure from your friends and other people?
What does it take to make responsible choices or your own decisions?
What help do you need in order to make decisions?
How can groups of youth make helpful decisions together?
What can you do to resist pressure if that is what is necessary?

Decisional Questions
How can you learn to recognize peer pressure?
What can individuals do to lessen negative peer pressure on them?
What do you plan to do about peer pressure in the future?

Discussing Discipline with a Student after a Confrontation

Designed for
Students

Situation
A seventh grade student has just punched another student beside his locker. The hall supervisor collars the student and takes him to the office. The teacher then has a conversation with the student.

Rational Objective
To help the student create an alternative to aggressive behavior to deal with a difficult situation.

Experiential Aim
To enable the student to take responsibility for his own choices.

The Conversation

Opening
OK, let's talk about what just happened.

Objective Questions
What happened, in sequence, please?
What did you do?
What did the other person do?
Who else was involved?
Who were the witnesses?

Reflective Questions
How did you feel after you acted this way?
How would you feel if someone did this to you?
Where have you seen this behavior before?

Interpretive Questions
What do you think promoted or caused the negative behavior?
What message does it send when you exhibit this kind of behavior?
What message do you want other people to have from you?
How could you have handled this differently?
Who could you have discussed the problem with?

Decisional Questions
When this situation comes up again, what can you do differently?
What consequences should you pay if you repeat this kind of mistake?

Closing
You are a very capable person, and I'm looking for some positive changes from you.

Debriefing a Major Trauma with Students or Staff

Designed for
Students

Situation
A traumatic incident has just happened in a high school. The immediate incident is over, but students and staff are shaken and need to talk about what has happened. Students go to their home-rooms for a conversation, led by the homeroom teacher.

Rational Aim
To talk about their personal experiences of the trauma. To face reality and begin to deal with it productively.

Experiential Aim
To move from shock to beginning to come to terms with the situation.

Hints
Some of these questions are difficult to answer, so if there are few spoken answers, don't worry. The very fact of raising these questions and following this flow allows deeper reflection later. It may be helpful to print out the questions for the students to take with them for solitary, small group, or family reflection.

The Conversation

Opening
This event has shaken all of us. Let's take a little time to reflect on what's happened, so we can come to terms with it. I'm going to ask some questions that will help us gradually process what happened. I would like you to let everyone have their own answers — no interrupting, arguing, or judging what anyone says.

Objective Questions
Imagine you were a video camera recording what you saw happening. What actions, words, phrases, objects, and scenes are recorded on your tape?
Let's get everything out so we all have a full picture of what happened.

Reflective Questions
What shocked you about this incident?
What was most frightening?
What made you want to escape?
How else did you find yourself reacting?
Any place you wanted to cheer?

Interpretive Questions
Why do you think this happened?
What might have been some other contributing factors?
What impact does it have on you?
How are you different now?
How might we be different a year from now?
What can we learn from this?

Decisional Questions
What can we do to prevent this from happening again?
Who else do you need to see or talk with?
What can we do to help each other now?
What can we do to symbolize how we changed or what we have learned?

Closing
We will undoubtedly continue to reflect on this. If you need help, please be sure to ask for it.

Debriefing a Conflict in Class

Designed for
Students

Situation
At the end of the day, a teacher decides to reflect on the conflict that happened in class earlier, so students can use the event as a learning experience.

Rational Aim
To enable students to develop a meaningful story about what happened and to know how to go on peacefully after a conflict.

Experiential Aim
To enable students to respect each other's views.

The Conversation

Opening
Remember when Jan and Mike got into a big fight earlier today?

Objective Questions
What words or phrases did you hear?
What did you see?

Reflective Questions
What part of this made you excited, angry, scared or worried?
What did this remind you of?

Interpretive Questions
What is different in our class now?
What story would you tell us about this event?

Decisional Questions
What change is needed?
How can we go on and make our class more peaceful?
What is the first action we need to take?

Closing
We can learn from events that happen, even the ones we don't like, if we reflect on them.

Examining Underachievement of Ethnic Groups in School

Designed for
Trustees

Situation
A study on underachievement of certain ethnic groups in a nearby urban school district has been reported in a newspaper article. The race relations consultant decides to discuss the article with trustees to catalyse some action in her school board.

Rational Aim
To understand the underachievement of ethnic groups and to arrive at a decision to deal with it.

Experiential Aim
To develop trust, understanding and empathy.

Hints
Pass out the paper or article, and then give a few minutes for people to read it. Ask them to note key points. This will be a highly sensitive topic. Language and word usage will be very important. It is critical to establish an atmosphere of respect right away. Ensuring that all affected groups are present and included in the discussion will be important.

Other Applications
Reviewing the implications of any article.

The Conversation

Opening
A study of the underachievement of some ethnic groups in a neighbouring board of education is reported in an article in the Saturday paper entitled "School System Fails Blacks, Portuguese." We may guess that a similar situation exists within our board. How can we address this problem? First of all, let's focus on the article: here's a copy. Take a little time to read it.

Objective Questions
What statistics in the article point to underachievement among Black and Portuguese students?
What statistics do we know about our own district?

Reflective Questions
What are your first reactions to this article?
Try to put yourself in the place of a Portuguese or black person. How do you feel about these findings?
What similar things does this remind you of in our school system?

Interpretive Questions
What are the long-term implications of under achievement of ethnic groups?
What lessons can we learn from this study?
What are the critical issues in our situation that need to be addressed?
How has this situation been addressed successfully in other locations?
What might be some solutions to this problem?

Decisional Questions
What do you think we can do to address this problem on an ongoing systematic basis?
Which one would make a difference for our minority students?
Which ones can we successfully implement?
Which of these suggestions should be given high priority?
What should be our next step?

Closing
Thank you. I hope this will move us a long way down the road to ensuring that all of our students achieve at the highest possible level.

Deciding on a Request for Exemption from an Exam

Designed for
Staff

Situation
A department of education has a strong rule that to receive the high school diploma, each student must pass the English exam. The department has received letters from a school principal and nurse asking that a particular student be exempted from the exam because of a recent suicide attempt. The department is concerned both about the student and about setting a precedent.

Rational Aim
To make an ethically appropriate decision.

Experiential Aim
To feel comfortable with the decision.
To feel able to handle similar situations in the future.

Hints
If it does not violate confidentiality protocols, each member should have a copy of the letters of request. It strengthens the objective level. Make sure that there are real answers to the other objective questions before the meeting as well. Listing implications of each possible decision on a flipchart or blackboard is probably useful, so that they are visually before the group as it makes its decision.

The Conversation

Opening
First let me read the letters of request aloud.

Objective Questions
Precisely what is being asked?
What factual information do we have about the student — records, grades, and history?
What are the official policies related to this?
What situations of this nature have come up in the past?
How have they been handled?

Reflective Questions
What is your first reaction about what to do?
What is the most difficult part of this decision?

Interpretive Questions
What are the underlying issues we need to address?
What might we be considering if this were our own child?
What would we need to consider if our own children were watching and learning from this example?
What are the other values, principles and policies that need to be considered?
Let's list some possible options for decisions that we could make.
Now let's evaluate each possible option with a few questions:
What are the positive and negative implications of each possible option?
What are the long term and short term benefits of the each option?
How does each option fit with the values, principles and policies we have identified?
How do the benefits of each of these decisions balance with the potential harms?
How does each option reflect our educational mission?
How would each of these be just or right for other students, given similar circumstances?
How does this decision consider the best interests of a particular student and the collective best interests of all students in our system?
How would you talk about the ethics of each option?

(continued)

Deciding on a Request for Exemption from an Exam *(continued)*

Decisional Questions

As you hear all of these values, what do you hear emerging as our decision?

How would you add to or refine this decision?

How do we need to communicate this decision?

What do we need to do (differently) for next time?

Closing

I know this is a difficult decision, but I really appreciate all the care that went into thinking it through. I'm sure others will understand the dilemma and how we have decided to deal with it.

Reviewing Requests to Cancel a Class Trip

Designed for
Teachers, Students and
Parents

Situation
An expensive school trip, traditional to the school, has been planned. A strong group of parents have objected that a number of families will find it a hardship to afford the trip. The school council has re-commended canceling it. Students and staff are upset, because they have been look-ing forward to the trip all year. The principal, vice-principal, and senior staff have to make the final decision. They are having the conversation with all the students, teachers, and parents.

Rational Aim
To make the final decision.

Experiential Aim
To experience that staff mem-bers care about everyone's feelings.

The Conversation

Opening
We need to make a decision regarding the field trip, and we all have to feel comfortable with it.

Objective Questions
Here is the information we have.
What questions of clarity do you have?
Are there any other facts that you know about this situation?

Reflective Questions
What's your initial response to this information?
What are your feelings surrounding this decision?

Interpretive Questions
What is it you really wanted to accomplish on this trip?
What are the implications if we cancel the trip? If we don't?
What else might we do that would accomplish the positive intent and minimize the negative impacts?

Decisional Questions
Given our feelings and the information, what should we do?
How should we communicate our decision to the rest of the parents, staff members, and students?

Closing
Given the situation, I believe we have made a choice we can live with.

Making Recommendations to Change the School Timetable

Designed for
Teachers and Staff

Situation
Due to required curriculum changes and budget cuts, the length of classes and number of classes per day have to be reduced. Teachers, students, and parents are anxious about the changes. The principal calls a meeting to discuss possibilities and come up with recommendations.

Rational Aim
To create a solution to the timetable issue.

Experiential Aim
To enable participants to take responsibility by creating solutions to a problem they resent.

Hints
A statement of the new requirements would be helpful at the objective level.
Small groups may work on possible solutions at the interpretive level, then bring them back to the group to discuss. Blank copies of a timetable would help people experiment with options. This task is difficult without graphics that depict the whole picture.
The decisional level may take some time, as people struggle with synthesis of the options. It may be necessary to assign a small group to take the results of the interpretive level and work them through, or to come back a day or so later with the whole group.

Other Applications
With minor adaptations, this can be used for other major changes that a group needs to work through.

The Conversation

Opening
We've got some major changes to make in our timetable that will affect all of us. We need all of our perspectives to come up with a workable solution.

Objective Questions
What are the characteristics of our present timetable?
How many classes do we cover each day? Minutes in each class?
What are the new requirements?

Reflective Questions
What makes you most anxious about the suggested changes?
What parts of the new situation are intriguing?

Interpretive Questions
What are the key differences between the old and the new requirements?
What are implications for the students? For teachers? For parents?
What are the bottom lines here?
What are possible ways to arrange our timetable to meet these requirements and best serve our students?
Let's look at each of these possible solutions:
What are the strengths and weaknesses of each?
What elements seem to work best?

Decisional Questions
How can we put these elements together to create a solution we can live with?

Closing
We'll flesh out this recommendation, and get back to you with the results.

Solving a Problem with Support Staff

Designed for
Staff

Situation
Several teachers have complained that their rooms have not been properly cleaned in the last few weeks. Rumors about budget cuts are rampant, and morale among support staff is low. The vice-principal is asked to have a conversation with the janitors about the situation.

Rational Aim
To make a decision about how to maintain a clean building.

Experiential Aim
To enable janitors to experience affirmation and support from administration despite the ambiguity of job cuts.

The Conversation

Opening
I've heard that some things are bothering you, and I've also noticed some uncharacteristically unfinished work in the last few weeks. I think we need to talk, because your work is important to the well being of students and their learning.

Objective Questions
What are some things that have happened in the last few weeks?
What are people talking about?

Reflective Questions
What is worrying you about our present situation?
What are you OK with, or even happy about?

Interpretive Questions
What are some of the underlying issues here?
How do these affect your work?
What are some possible responses to these issues?

Decisional Questions
What can we do to deal with these issues and make sure the work gets done?

Closing
Thank you for your honesty. We'll all try to make sure these things happen. When shall we talk again?

Involving Staff in School Improvement Planning

Designed for
Teachers and Staff

Situation
A mandated School Improvement Plan (SIP) at an elementary school has been running for a year, but with little staff participation. It needs to be revised, and invigorated with more participation from teachers. The SIP committee has asked for twenty minutes at a staff meeting to discuss it.

Rational Aim
To create a revised action plan for school improvement.

Experiential Aim
To be committed to being involved in the School Improvement Plan.

The Conversation

Opening
We need to come together and talk about the School Improvement Plan.

Objective Questions
What aspects of the SIP have you seen implemented this year?

Reflective Questions
What are your immediate reactions to the SIP?

Interpretive Questions
What part of the SIP do you see as most important to you?
What parts of this are workable? Which parts don't work well?
What are the purposes of the SIP?
How could the SIP help make our school more effective?

Decisional Questions
What can we do individually to help make this more effective?
What component of the SIP are you willing to be involved in?

Closing
We can see from this conversation that for our school to be more effective, it is vital for everyone to be involved in the School Improvement Plan. I'm glad you are willing to be a part of it.

Thinking through a Serious Personnel Issue

Designed for
Teachers and Staff

Situation
An administrator is having difficulty with a tenured teacher. This conversation is one the administrator has with herself to clarify how to deal with the teacher.

Rational Aim
To decide how to move forward on a serious personnel issue.

Experiential Aim
To develop the courage to move.

Hints
If the first step is to talk with someone else, a similar set of questions can be used with them.

The Conversation

Opening
I am going to address a serious personnel issue. This reflective conversation is the first step.

Objective Questions
What facts do I know about this situation?
What employment history is relevant here?
What behaviors have been observed or reported regarding this teacher?
What have I seen myself?

Reflective Questions
What is my reaction or response to these reports?
What is my real concern about this? Why?

Interpretive Questions
What are my legal obligations?
What are the possible traps or dangers in making a decision in this situation?
What are my options?
What are the advantages and disadvantages of each option?
How do these options impact students? — Parents? Other teachers?

Decisional Questions
What do I need to verify with other teachers, parents, or students?
What's my first step?

Closing
OK. Let's do it.

Exploring the Concept of Effective Teams

Designed for
Teachers and Staff

Situation
A principal wants her staff to be organized in teams, to share responsibility for the life of the school. She leads a conversation in a staff meeting to prepare teachers for the idea.

Rational Objective
To explore ways that teamwork can help teachers.

Experiential Aim
To experience anticipation of better teamwork.

The Conversation

Opening
Effective schools are based on the development of effective teams. So we want to spend a little time discussing, "What is an effective team?"

Objective Questions
Where have you seen effective teams working? Give examples.
What are other examples of effective teamwork? In society? History? Sport? Any others?

Reflective Questions
What can be frustrating about working with a team?
What do you enjoy about teamwork?
When have you wished for more teamwork among our staff?

Interpretive Questions
What are the results or benefits of effective teamwork?
What could we do better here with team effort?
What elements are needed to create a good team?
What are some of the requirements for an effective team? What must be in place?
How would you determine who needs to be a member of a team?
How would you determine roles and responsibilities?
What impact might teamwork have on our program?

Decisional Questions
What is the first thing you want to try to tackle in teams?

Closing
The next time we talk we need to focus on how we can organize teams and what guidelines we will need to guide them.

Identifying Challenges with Discipline

Designed for
Teachers and Staff

Situation
A school consultant starts an in-service session with teachers with this conversation to identify challenges with discipline. It is done before a workshop on realistic strategies to deal with these discipline challenges.

Rational Aim
To understand the underlying challenges of discipline in the school.

Experiential Aim
To experience dealing with problems within a larger context of affirmation.

Hints
Simple procedures for a workshop method based on the steps of the conversation method are included in the appendix.

Other Applications
Similar conversations can be used to look for underlying obstacles for other problems.

The Conversation

Opening
In a few minutes, we are going to do a workshop on realistic strategies to deal with discipline problems. In order to do that, we need to get a clearer picture of what is behind the challenges we have. Let's start with a few simple questions.

Objective Questions
What is an example of a discipline problem that you have encountered recently?

Reflective Questions
What other situations in your teaching experience are you reminded of?
What is the most difficult part of these challenges?

Interpretive Questions
What sustains this behavior?
What are some of the factors behind discipline problems at our school?
Why do these underlying factors continue to exist?
What strategies for dealing with discipline have worked in the past?
What has not worked as well as you would like?
Why do you think these strategies have or have not worked?
What does this say about the underlying obstacles that sustain these problems?

Decisional Questions
How would you summarize what we've said here?

Closing
Next we are going to do a workshop on realistic strategies to deal with these problems.

Responding to a Proposed School Leadership Change

Designed for
Teachers and Staff

Situation
The school board has announced that it is moving both the principal and the vice-principal at the same time next year. The advisory council has called an emergency meeting to discuss the issue.

Rational Aim
To decide on a response to the announcement.

Experiential Aim
To sense the power of the advisory council to affect school changes.

The Conversation

Opening
As you all know, we are losing our principal and vice principal at the same time. We need to look the situation over and take our concerns to the board.

Objective Questions
Think back to the last time that a principal or vice-principal was moved from this school. When was that?
What happened when one of them moved?

Reflective Questions
What worked well in the past in relation to administrative changes?
What hasn't?
What is your immediate reaction about losing both principal and vice-principal?
What angers you?
What doors might this open for us?

Interpretive Questions
How do you feel this will affect the school community?
What might be some positive effects?
What could be negative effects?
What values do we want to see honored in this decision?

Decisional Questions
How shall we respond?
What are we going to do to get our opinion heard?
How will we present our response?

Closing
This plan will make our concerns known. We have certainly taken a major step in making our concerns known about the school climate that affects our children's learning. Thank you very much for your concern and creativity.

Discussing Homophobia

Designed for
Teachers and Staff

Situation
A consultant is doing in-service training for teachers to break down homophobia in the schools. George, a gay student, has just given a personal presentation on his experience.

Rational Aim
To understand the effects of homophobia on students.

Experiential Aim
To experience compassion for gays in the school and commitment to changing hateful behavior.

Hints
People will likely come into a conversation like this with opinions already formed. Keeping the focus on the speaker's presentation until well into the interpretive level will be important to increase the likelihood that participants see the situation from a new perspective. The facilitator may have to work hard to make sure that people actually answer the questions that are asked. It may be helpful to have the questions written out where people can see them all as they go through the conversation.

Other Applications
This may be used to explore individual presentations from other marginalized groups.

The Conversation

Opening
Let's take a little time to explore George's experience and its implications.

Objective Questions
What is one thing you heard the speaker say?
What were the events he described?
What people did he mention?
What words or phrases caught your attention?
What feelings did he identify?
What other points did the speaker make — for example, strategies, recommendations, or guidelines for relating to gay people?

Reflective Questions
What popped into your mind when we introduced the speaker?
What impressions came to your mind as he spoke?
What did you find interesting?
What concerns came to you?
How do you relate to how he felt?
What details of George's experience can you relate to?
Can you describe a situation similar to this?

Interpretive Questions
What were the most significant things that happened to George?
Why did this happen? What roadblocks were there? Supports?
What are some of the issues homosexual students face generally? In the school system?
What are the implications for teachers and schools?
What have you learned from this conversation?

Decisional Questions
What changes are needed to make this a place where people are respected?
What strategies can we apply in the classroom, the hallway, the playground, the staff room, and the community?
What are you committed to do?
What are our next steps?

Closing
When we work together like this, we can make the world a better place for the diversity of its people.

Dealing with Inappropriate Conduct at Recess

Designed for
Teachers and Staff

Situation
In a staff meeting, teachers are discussing ways of dealing with inappropriate student conduct at recess.

Rational Aim
To learn effective ways to prevent and deal with inappropriate behavior.

Experiential Aim
To experience a shift from reacting to events to being able to be proactive.

The Conversation

Objective Questions
What type of conduct are you seeing at recess?
What strategies have you tried to correct these?
How frequently do you intervene?

Reflective Questions
What was an intervention that made you feel effective.
What was one where you felt ineffective or unsatisfied with the results?
What would the "perfect" recess look like?

Interpretive Questions
What patterns did you notice from these stories?
What factors seem to be critical in dealing with student conduct effectively?

Decisional Questions
How can we integrate these critical factors into our schoolyard routines?
What changes do we need to make as a staff?
How can we accomplish these changes?

Closing
Let's continue to share our wisdom and experience on tough issues like this. We can all learn a lot from each other.

Reflecting on a Rough Day on the Way Home

Designed for
Teachers and Staff

Situation
A teacher has had a really rough day, enough to burn anyone out. He is driving home after work and desperately needs to process the day so as not to ruin his evening. He decides to have a disciplined conversation with himself, to reflect on what happened.

Rational Aim
To glean the learnings from the day

Experiential Aim
To affirm the events of the day in real life

Hints
Conversations in one's own head are the hardest to keep on track. The emphasis is on the experiential aim, rather than the content.

Other Applications
Try using this structure for daily journal writing. A commuter might talk into a small cassette recorder. The conversation also works well for students to reflect on the day to consolidate their learnings, or for anyone to learn from the experience of a difficult event.

The Conversation

Opening
OK, let me focus on this day for a moment.

Objective Questions
What were the things that happened today?
What did I do?
What did the kids do?
What other things happened?

Reflective Questions
Which parts of this day were the most frustrating? Made me mad?
What parts were the tiniest bit hopeful or a little fun?

Interpretive Questions
What have I learned about what works with teaching today?
What have I learned about what doesn't work?
In the big picture of things, what is the importance of today?
How does this affect what I'll do in the future?

Decisional Questions
What metaphor or poetic title would sum up this day?

Closing
Whew, now I can leave this day behind and not take it home with me.

Talking with Teachers about a Frustrating Field Trip

Designed for
Teachers and Staff

Situation
A group of teachers have taken a large number of students, including some children with disabilities, to a puppet show. They have encountered a number of obstacles and have come back upset. The team leader decides to lead a conversation to debrief the experience.

Rational Aim
To learn from the frustrations of this field trip.

Experiential Aim
To share the experience and let go of the frustrations.

Hints
When a group is really upset about something, leave enough time at the reflective level to get the frustrations spoken, but then move the group past them with interpretive questions. This will keep the group from getting stuck in negative emotion and help them move forward.

The Conversation

Opening
We want to go over the events of this theater trip in order to prevent these problems on future trips.

Objective Questions
Describe the puppet show setting.
What obstacles to accessibility did we encounter?
What were the children's responses?

Reflective Questions
What were the various feelings throughout the trip?
Where in your body did you feel your frustration?
Describe what it felt like.

Interpretive Questions
What can we learn from this experience?

Decisional Questions
What will we do differently next time?
What suggestions will we make to other teachers?

Closing
It's helpful to get perspective on these kinds of situations and learn from them.

Exploring Alternatives to Punitive Discipline

Designed for
Teachers and Staff

Situation
A group of teachers has decided that the emphasis on punishment in their school is not decreasing disruptive behavior. They decide to explore alternatives.

Rational Objective
To come up with new ideas about turning behavior around.

Experiential Aim
To generate hope and new energy for dealing with discipline.

Hints
To sustain the hope and fresh insight generated by this conversation, there should be a follow-up conversation a month or so afterward to reflect on changes, and learn from experience.

The Conversation

Opening
We want to discuss what creative ways we can use to deal with discipline.

Objective Questions
Where have you seen examples of negative behaviors?

Reflective Questions
What effect has this behavior had on others?

Interpretive Questions
How do we let disruptive students know that their behavior is a problem?
How can we discover what the child is good at and bring that out?
What are ways we can have the class work as a team to support the best and redirect the worst behaviors?

Decisional Questions
What are actions we could implement to enable changes in behavior to become more positive?

Closing
This is just initiating our thinking about what is possible to turn around behavior from negative to positive.

Increasing Teacher Skills in Effective Discipline

Designed for
Teachers and Staff

Situation
A principal of a school with a number of newer teachers is concerned with the number of discipline problems being sent to the office. A staff meeting is designated to discuss the issue.

Rational Aim
To discuss how to teachers can more effectively discipline their own students without needing to rely on others.

Experiential Aim
To increase teachers' confidence in applying discipline methods successfully.

The Conversation

Opening
Discipline is difficult when it goes beyond the classroom and involves other adults. We want to share ways to handle more of the discipline problems ourselves and support others' attempts.

Objective Questions
What are some examples of misbehavior taking place recently?
Who is usually present? Who is involved?
What are some of the standards in the classrooms agreed upon before incidents occur?
What are some steps you take when it does take place?

Reflective Questions
How do participants feel when outbreaks occur?
How does the rest of the class feel?
What is your biggest concern?

Interpretive Questions
How do these incidents affect the classroom?
What is at the root of the problem? At what levels? Why?
What are some examples of classroom management techniques that have actually worked for you?
What rules do you think are important to have?

Decisional Questions
How can we get the students involved in solving discipline problems?
What changes will you make in your classroom?
What school-wide changes would you like to see?
What kind of support do you need?
How will we involve all parties?

Closing
We have discussed what problems exist, how these problems come about, and what exacerbates them. We also talked about reactions to them. The most important thing is that we have decided on some steps that can prevent these problems in the future. Working together like this is going to help us more effectively solve these problems.

Discussing Strategy for a Student's Misbehavior as a Faculty

Designed for
Teachers and Staff

Situation
It has come to the attention of several teachers that the misbehavior of one student is having a strong effect on the whole school, and needs to be dealt with in a caring manner.

Rational Objective
To discuss specific situations of misbehavior of a particular student, notice any patterns of good behavior, and to create a team response.

Experiential Aim
To experience caring, understanding and empathy for the student.

The Conversation

Opening
It has come to our attention that students and teachers are concerned about Johnny's behavior.

Objective Questions
What specific acts of misbehavior have you seen in the classroom? In the halls? On the playground?
When have you found him behaving well?

Reflective Questions
How does this student antagonize others?
What is it that upsets other students and parents the most?
What worries you the most about his behavior?

Interpretive Questions
Which behaviors have the most negative impact for this student and for other students?
How does the misbehavior affect the instructional program?
How does his behavior affect relations with students, teachers, and parents?
What may be some of the causes of this behavior?
Where do you see chinks in the armor, or places that are vulnerable to outside influence?
What values do we want to hold the next time that he has a problem?

Decisional Questions
What might we do to limit the destructive behavior and encourage positive behavior?
When shall we come back and evaluate how our plan is working?
How would you make this a learning experience for others?

Closing
How we handle these situations affects everyone. The community around a child gives messages to a child that have an impact on his behavior. When we act together, we can strengthen the impact we have.

Dealing with Complaints about a Staff Member

Designed for
Teachers and Staff

Situation
Several parents have come to the principal with serious complaints about a teacher from their students in a grade seven class. The principal is concerned that the situation be dealt with carefully and fairly, protecting both the students and the teacher. First the principal interviews all involved individually and documents what they say. Each interview is confidential, so that there is a safe environment to speak.

Rational Aim
To understand the situation and receive input on what to do.

Experiential Aim
To diffuse feelings and develop the capacity to look for positive solutions.

Hints
Setting out the questions where participants can see all of them before answering helps to create safety in answering, and also allows people to hold answers until the question comes up. Depending on the situation, this conversation may be followed by the justice circle conversation (see Chapter 10), which puts everyone together to resolve and heal the situation.

The Conversation

Opening
As my memo to invite you to this interview states, some serious allegations have been made about this teacher. Before we proceed any further, we need to establish the facts. In the end, it is my responsibility to make a decision about what to do next, but I want to be really clear about what happened so far, and I want to hear from all perspectives. I will also be interviewing others. Everything said is strictly confidential. These are the questions I will be asking.

Objective Questions
Tell me what has been going on with this teacher. Try to speak from the standpoint of an external reporter, holding a video recorder. Be as specific as you can.
Give me a specific example or two of the teacher's actions, as best you can.
What are some things that may have led up to this?

Reflective Questions
What part of this situation has been the most upsetting to you?
What worries you the most?
What frightens you?

Interpretive Questions
What do you think might be behind this?
Why do you think this is happening?
What implications do you see for the students? The teacher? Others?
Which elements of school policies does this invoke?

Decisional Questions
What are your thoughts on what we might do to deal with this situation?
What are we obliged to do?
What else do you recommend?

Closing
Thank you for your input. As I said at the beginning, I am gathering all the information I can on this situation, and I will be making a decision as soon as I have conclusive data.

Handling an Irate Phone Call

Designed for
Teachers and Staff

Situation
The school secretary has just answered the phone. A parent identifies herself and begins almost immediately to shout incoherently. The secretary must find out about the situation in order to decide who should deal with it.

Rational Aim
To discover the real problem.

Experiential Aim
To have the parent calm down and experience being taken seriously.

Hints
The secretary can take notes in order to give the next person a "briefing". A notepad can even be printed up to take these notes, since the irate person may not answer the questions in order! A sample can be found in the appendix.

Other Applications
Not only secretaries get irate phone calls! Parents, administrators, and teachers also get them or have people come into their offices upset. Anyone can use sequence of questions to guide the conversation.

The Conversation

Opening
Ms. Jones, please wait just a minute. I'm having difficulty understanding you. I need to understand you better in order to help you.

Objective Questions
Could you start at the beginning and tell me what happened?
What happened after that?
What have you tried to do?

Reflective Questions
You sound really upset. When did you first feel there was a problem?
What's the worst part of this for you?

Interpretive Questions
What do you think is causing this?
What are the implications?
What would help resolve the situation?

Decisional Questions
What are you recommending?
Who would you like to speak with about this?

Closing
Could you please hold while I see if this person is available to help you?

Talking With a Parent about a Child with Discipline Problems

Designed for
Parents and Community

Situation
A child in the school has suddenly begun acting aggressively, disrupting her class and the playground. The teacher is concerned, and makes an appointment with the parent.

Rational Aim
To understand Molly's behavior, and create a plan to care for her.

Experiential Aim
To increase trust and respect between teacher and parent

Hints
When the facilitator has an opinion or some answers to his own questions, it is difficult for the other participants not to feel that the facilitator is trying to manipulate the conversation to his own ends. Be very careful when you insert an answer or an opinion, that you make it clear when shifting hats between discussion leader and participant.

The Conversation

Opening
I've asked you to come because I'm worried about Molly. Generally, she's always behaved in a pretty normal fashion, but in the past month she's begun acting very aggressively, jumping up from her seat and hitting other children. I wonder what's going on and what we can do about it.

Objective Questions
What have you noticed Molly doing in the last month or so?
What new or different behaviors have you observed?
What, if any, changes have there been in your family situation that might affect Molly's behavior?
What have been some of the other changes that you have noticed in Molly's life?

Reflective Questions
What part of this worries you the most about Molly's situation?
What part are you relatively unconcerned about?

Interpretive Questions
What do you think might be some of the causes of this change in behavior?

Decisional Questions
What might we do about it as the school? As her family?
What are you committed to?
The school is committed to _____.
How can we make sure we're successful?

Closing
When we work together, we can make a difference, and I'm glad we can start right away. We all want Molly to succeed.

Discussing a Response to Education Cutbacks

Designed for
Parents and Community

Situation
Cutbacks in school funding are imminent, and children (students) will be affected. Parents have called an emergency meeting to discuss what to do.

Rational Aim
To develop a thought-through response to the cutbacks.

Experiential Aim
To enable parents to move from helplessness and anger to commitment and hope.

Hints
When a group comes in ready to vent, it is difficult to move them beyond the reflective level. This conversation must be led by a strong facilitator. The conversation will build on participants' reactions, and take them beyond venting to responsible action.

The Conversation

Opening
We have called this meeting to clarify the new budget cutbacks, our reactions to them, and to decide how to respond. This is the detailed announcement of the cutbacks. Let's start by seeing just what it says.

Objective Questions
What facts catch your attention here?
What other information do you have about the cutbacks?

Reflective Questions
What parts of this are most alarming?
What parts are you okay with?

Interpretive Questions
What are the likely results of this new situation, both positive and negative?
What would tell us that these are positive results or negative results?
What would be the implications of leaving funding as is, both positive and negative?
What seem to be our overriding concerns here?

Decisional Questions
What changes would deal with the concerns about cutbacks and also the negative implications of leaving funding as is?
What can we do to respond to these concerns?
Who will do these things?

Closing
There is a quote attributed to Margaret Mead that says, "Never doubt that a small group of thoughtful, committed citizens can change the world. Indeed, it's the only thing that ever has." We can make a difference if we focus our efforts.

Leading an Inspirational Study to Begin a Board Meeting

Designed for
Parents and Community

Situation
At the beginning of each board meeting of a child center, different board members take turns leading an inspirational study. One such discussion is beginning.

Rational Aim
To think about roles and different perspectives.

Experiential Aim
To make a transition to thoughtfulness and focus on the meeting at hand.
To reinvigorate the childcare center board members.

Hints
Choose a quote or reading that is appropriate to the group or the situation. Keep the conversation moving quickly, but don't be afraid of silence. Sometimes only one or two answers for each question are enough to transform the mood of the group.

Other Applications
This is a useful tool for any group that is distracted, tired or dispirited. Uplifting passages help the group make a transition from their individual regular workday tasks to the common work of caring for the school. The topics can range from meditations from various daily spiritual journals, thoughtful papers, relevant news articles, and favorite one-line quotes.

The Conversation

Opening
The convenor reads the following vignette from *Chicken Soup for the Soul:*

> Roles—and How We Play Them
> Whenever I'm disappointed with my spot in life, I stop and think about little Jamie Scott. Jamie was trying out for a part in a school play. His mother told me that he had his heart set on being in it, though she feared he would not be chosen. On the day the parts were announced, I went with her to collect him after school. Jamie rushed up to her, eyes shining with pride and excitement. "Guess what, mum," He shouted. And then said those words that remain a lesson to me. "I've been chosen to clap and cheer." — Marie Curling

Objective Questions
Who were the characters in the story?

Reflective Questions
Which person did you identify with?

Interpretive Questions
When have you found yourself playing a role you did not expect, but realized was important?

Decisional Questions
As educators, how can we encourage the people and children we work with to discover their perfect "role" and "chosen" part?

Closing
Let's keep our reflections from this conversation in mind as we continue with board business this evening.

Understanding the State of the School

Designed for
Parents and Community

Situation
Existing board members of a small non-profit preschool, which has undergone substantial financial, legal, personnel, and administrative crises over the last several months, are meeting to reflect on their current situation and discover where to go in the next year.

Rational Objective
To arrive at a clear, common understanding of where the school is and what is needed, and who is committed to help strengthen the school.

Experiential Aim
To develop commitment to going forward and willingness to work as a team

Hints
When participants have "questions of clarity" at the objective level, the reporter or someone on their team can answer with facts, or simply say, "I don't have an answer". The facilitator of the conversation keeps both the questions and the answers objective.

The Conversation

Opening
Let's start by giving five-minute reports on problems and topics you're working on, such as various aspects of finances, enrollment, events, and staffing. Please include the facts of what happened and insights that were revealed. This will give everyone a picture of the "State of the School."

Objective Questions
What words or phrases did you hear in these reports?
What questions of clarity do you want to ask the reporters?

Reflective Questions
Which parts of these reports made your heart sing or lifted your spirits?
What parts made you want to cry or run away?
Where did you find yourself puzzled or stunned?
Where did you breathe a sigh of relief?

Interpretive Questions
What gifts do we have as a school?
Where did you sense gaps — a need not being met, a task uncompleted, a situation not dealt with, or an unexplored opportunity?
What are the key challenges we are currently facing?
As you listened to the reports, what insights into our situation came to you?
If you were to describe this moment in our history as a turning point, what are we turning from? What are we turning toward?
Having heard the state of the school described, what directions do we need to take?
What opportunities do we need to explore?

Decisional Questions
What actions do we need to take to meet our stated plans?
How are you willing to commit to the school at this point?
If so, what will be your contribution?

Closing
I feel that, as a result of this conversation, everyone has a better view of where the school is, what we need and where we, as individual trustees, are committed to going forward. Thank you.

Recommending Appropriate Consequences for Inappropriate Behavior

Designed for
Parents and Community

Situation
Parents on the school council are concerned about students' behavior, and want to make some recommendations for school policy. This conversation is held at a school council meeting.

Rational Aim
To list behaviors and recommended consequences.

Experiential Aim
To experience having been heard and affecting the school in a positive way.

Hints
This is a direct approach that is not addressing the deeper questions of looking for systemic solutions. It is an effective conversation, but it is only part of the real solution. Another conversation on systemic solutions may also be held.

The Conversation

Opening
This discussion is about behaviors that are not acceptable and what consequences should apply.

Objective Questions
What are some unacceptable behaviors you have seen or heard about recently in our school? Describe the situation in some detail.

Reflective Questions
What words, phrases, or incidents stuck in your mind from these stories?
What is your reaction when a child comes to you about an incident that happened at school with another child?
What did other people say that rings a bell with you?

Interpretive Questions
Why do you think these problems are occurring?
What are the inappropriate behaviors you would like to see dealt with quickly?
What are possible consequences for each of these behaviors?
What are values we want to hold in choosing the appropriate consequences for each behavior?

Decisional Questions
Which of these consequences should we choose for each of these behaviors?
Which of these are priorities?
How do you inform the school community about these decisions?

Closing
We would like to present the school administration with a list of misbehaviors and a corresponding list of recommended consequences. Hopefully the recommendations will be implemented as soon as possible with approval of the school administration.

Solving a Safety Problem

Designed for
Parents and Community

Situation
Concerns have been voiced about traffic safety around the elementary school. The parent council is discussing the problems.

Rational Aim
To create a plan for improving traffic safety around the school.

Experiential Aim
To enable parents to come away knowing that the children will be safer. To experience working together on a problem.

The Conversation

Opening
People have come to me with concerns about the traffic safety around the school. This meeting has been called to talk about this and make some changes before someone is hurt or killed.

Objective Questions
When you observe our children coming to school and leaving it, what are some problems you have seen?
What are previously reported problems you have heard about?

Reflective Questions
Which of these problems worries you the most?

Interpretive Questions
What are the underlying problems that need to be addressed?

Decisional Questions
What can we do in order to improve this situation?
What will these measures cost in money and time?
How will we pay for them?
How can we involve the students in improving the situation?
Who will make sure these things happen?

Closing
Parents have had the chance to voice their fears and concerns about school traffic safety. We will all work together to create a safer area for the children.

CHAPTER 9

Evaluating Learning

The conversations in this chapter provide a variety of ways to assess learning. These conversations assume that the intention of evaluation is to ascertain the quality of learning and to see how behavior has changed as a result of that learning. They do not try to rate the quantity of material that has been assimilated, although they may be used to assess the meaning of quantitative results, and plan a response to them.

Participants in these conversations may be students, teachers, administrators, or parents, or a combination of them. Note that some of the conversations are designed to be led by students or parents, and some by teachers or administrators.

Evaluating a Program with Preschoolers

Designed for
Students

Situation
The funder of a multi-cultural neighbourhood preschool wants the students to evaluate their program.

Rational Aim
To obtain feedback from students on the impact of their program

Experiential Aim
To experience delight in sharing

Hints
Although most conversations use language, there are many ways to communicate ideas and answers. This conversation uses kinesthetic (body movement) and visual-spatial intelligences in addition to language to answer questions so that young children with limited verbal expression can communicate in a wider variety of ways.
For people with difficulty in understanding a question or those who have a narrow range of verbal expression, giving a broad range of possible answers may help them to choose their answer. Make sure you are not just giving prompts for the answers you want to hear!

Other Applications
Although this conversation is quite specific, the ways of asking for responses may be used with other groups with limited language, such as special education classes or ESL classes.

The Conversation

Objective Questions
What did you do today? Show me some things you do in preschool — either point to a toy or act out an activity you do.

Reflective Questions
What do you like to do here? Bring me your favourite thing to play with.
When do you ever feel sad, angry, or unhappy here? Show me what it looks like.

Interpretive Questions
What is something you've learned to do here? Point to something that you've learned to do.

Decisional Questions
Draw me a picture of the best part of preschool. Can you tell me about your picture?
May I write what you said on the picture?

Closing
Thank you for sharing with me.

Reflecting on a Spelling Bee

Designed for
Students

Situation
A grade six class has participated in a district-wide spelling bee. No student advanced to the next level, and the mood is low.

Rational Aim
To realize that competition sometimes doesn't seem fair, yet learning can take place even when you lose.

Experiential Aim
To experience the joy and pain, and to be aware of other people's feelings

The Conversation

Opening
Let's reflect on our experience of being in the competition.

Objective Questions
What were some of the words we had to spell?

Reflective Questions
What were easy words?
Which words were difficult?
How did you feel when you spelled a word correctly?
How did you feel when you misspelled a word?
How did you feel when others got the same word right?
How do you suppose others felt when you succeeded or failed in spelling a word?

Interpretive Questions
What did you learn about spelling from this experience?
What did you learn about succeeding at spelling the words correctly?
What did you learn about coming up with the right spelling when you are unsure?
What did you learn about being in a public competition?
What did you learn about dealing with stress?
What did you learn about winning and losing?
Why do you think we participated in the spelling bee?
What did you / we gain from this experience?

Decisional Questions
How will you use what you've learned about winning and losing in other situations?
How will you prepare for next year's spelling bee?

Closing
Winning is great at the moment, but learning lasts for the rest of our lives.
You are great students.

Coaching a Sports Team

Designed for
Students

Situation
The coach of a girls' baseball team has the whole team reflect on each game for a few minutes right after the game.

Rational Aim
To conclude the game as a team

Experiential Aim
To encourage players to aspire to higher levels of play. To give confidence and affirm players' identity and worth in the team

Hints
Tailor the questions carefully for both the sport and the results of the game.
The Interpretive and Decisional questions may require probing and grounding questions. Focus on the positive for motivation.

Other Situations
Conversations similar to this may be used before a game or after a practice.

The Conversation

Objective Questions
What was the score?
How many runs did we make?
What happened in the game?
What is one thing you saw or heard from where you were playing?

Reflective Questions
When did you get really excited?
When were you discouraged or feel badly?

Interpretive Questions
What did we really do well? Why?
What could we have done better at? Give an example.

Decisional Questions
What are we going to do differently next time?
What are you personally going to do differently next time?
If you were to do this game again and make one outstanding play, what would you do?

Closing
All right! I really enjoy working with you. See you at practice.

Reflecting With Students on an Enrichment Program

Designed for
Students

Situation
Eighth grade students have participated in a part-time enrichment program for the past year. District staff would like to get their feedback as part of their decision about whether to continue the program.

Rational Aim
To enable students to think through their experiences in the enrichment program and provide feedback for future program planning.

Experiential Aim
To take pride in their accomplishments and realize that their experience can be applied to future learning.

The Conversation

Opening
We would like to help you think about your experience in the enrichment program and get your ideas about how to run such programs in the future.

Objective Questions
Which parts of the program do you remember most?
What other work did you do?
What work did you do outside the classroom?

Reflective Questions
What were the highlights of the program for you?
What was surprising for you?
What work went easily?
What was more difficult than you expected?
What did you feel the most proud of?
What do you wish you had done better?

Interpretive Questions
What problems did you find?
What skills did you learn here that will help you in the future?
What would you have liked to experience that was not part of this program?
What will you tell other students they will learn if they apply to get into the program next year?
What goal would you set for yourself if you did another enrichment program?

Decisional Questions
What skills or other learning have you developed that will help you in your regular class work?
How would you respond if we told you we would not be able to continue the program?
What reasons would you give for finding a way to continue the program?
Who do you think should participate in the program?
What changes would you recommend? What ideas do you have about next steps we should take to run the program next year?

Closing
I'm really glad to have you a part of the program. Thank you for your insights. We'll let you know what happens.

Sharing Use of Portfolios for Student Assessment

Designed for
Teachers and Staff Members

Situation
A school is holding an in-service on the use of portfolios of student work to strengthen student self-assessment and goal setting.

Rational Aim
To develop an understanding of the purpose of the portfolio. To share strategies to help students self-assess their work

Experiential Aim
To deepen commitment to portfolios and decrease frustration about their use.

The Conversation

Opening
Let's take some time to share how we've used portfolios and other assessment strategies.

Objective Questions
What subject portfolios do you have at present?
What is in these portfolios?
Can you share some ways you have kids self-assess key pieces of work — this could be a math problem-solving activity, a poem, a piece of art, etc.?
How do you actually use them?

Reflective Questions
What have you struggled with in the use of portfolios?
Where have you had a big "aha!" happen in relation to their use?

Interpretive Questions
Why do we keep portfolios?
What is the value of the portfolio?
When assessing their work, what do kids need to focus on?
What are the best practices in using portfolios in the classroom?
What resources will support the use of portfolios for assessment?

Decisional Questions
How can we help parents and kids value the portfolio?

Closing
Thank you, I think we have all learned a lot we can put to good use.

Evaluating a Library Program

Designed for
Teachers and Staff Members

Situation
A pilot book exchange program has been going for a few months. The librarian in the media center has taken stock and discovered chaos. Lots of late returns and lost books are rapidly depleting the choices. The librarian asks for a discussion at the staff meeting.

Rational Aim
To decrease overdue books and material losses in the media center.

Experiential Aim
To build shared responsibility for the book exchange program.

Hints
The final question will require some discussion to select actions that can and will be implemented by the participants. There may be some negotiation toward a set of actions that will actually do the job.

The Conversation

Opening
We hold both scheduled class exchanges and unscheduled small group or individual exchanges. There have been many losses of books, and we need to evaluate this program.

Objective Questions
What are some examples of how your students have used this program?
What behaviors have you observed in the students?

Reflective Questions
What reactions are you getting from your students?
What is an example of when it went well?
What are some examples of where book exchange was a disaster?
What difficulties do you see in the library with book exchange?

Interpretive Questions
Why do you think we have so many late returns and losses?
What routines are not working?
Where do you think the problem lies?

Decisional Questions
What can we do to improve our library book exchanges?
What are the key next steps? For the library staff? For teachers?

Closing
Thank you. I think this will help keep the books circulating to everyone's benefit. We'll check on this again at the next staff meeting.

Sharing Techniques of Evaluation and Assessment

Designed for
Teachers and Staff Members

Situation
A brief in-service training has been set up to expand staff knowledge of evaluation and assessment techniques. Since there is a wide range of experience among teachers, it has been decided that no outside expert is required. Teachers have been asked to bring an example of a successful evaluation strategy.

Rational Aim
To explore various evaluation and assessment techniques, and to learn new techniques.

Experiential Aim
To increase respect for each other's knowledge.

The Conversation

Objective Questions
What is one evaluation and/or assessment strategy that you use in your classroom — could you describe it succinctly or draw a quick diagram to explain it?
Are there any questions about how that works?
Someone else…

Reflective Questions
Which aspects of evaluation and assessment do you find most difficult or most frustrating?
Which aspects do you find most helpful, useful or successful?
What do you see that "works" or really shows promise?

Interpretive Questions
What are some similarities you noticed among the methods we shared?
What are some of the differences?
What aspects of the assessment strategies make them effective?
What have you learned this afternoon that you will be able to use in your classroom?

Decisional Questions
How will you use it?
How can we support each other in making assessment and evaluation effective in our classrooms?

Closing
We've learned some really important things this afternoon. Thank you for all your wisdom!

Evaluating School Achievement Data

Designed for
Teachers and Staff Members

Situation
The government has mandated school improvement action planning based on the results of standardized tests of school achievement. School staff must evaluate the significance of the test results, prioritize effective strategies to improve school performance, and act on those strategies.

Rational Aim
To identify priorities for improvement in school performance.

Experiential Aim
To engender commitment to improvement and the hope that it will work.

Hints
The opening reading may be done in small groups, highlighting relevant facts. A "jigsaw method" may be used where small groups focus on certain sections of the data, then share observations. The objective level questions can focus on one section of data at a time, then repeat for the next section.
At the interpretive and decisional levels, write the answers on the board or a flipchart so that the information is available to the group for the next questions.
In this conversation, there will be a tendency to want to answer reflective and interpretive questions as soon as the reading is done. This may lead to defensiveness rather than thoughtful evaluation.
(continued)

The Conversation

Opening
Here are summaries of relevant school data for everyone. This includes school achievement data from standardized testing, data from student and home questionnaires, board and provincial data, report card data, and some other relevant school and/or achievement data such as exemplars or representative student portfolios.
Let's take a short time to skim through the data, and then I am going to ask the questions I have posted on the board. We will focus on facts first, then connections and responses, then interpretation, and finally implications for action.

Objective Questions
What data catches your eye in each of these categories?
What facts stand out?
What questions of clarity do you have?
What is unclear to you?

Reflective Questions
What surprises you in this information?
What most concerns you?
How does this data compare with your intuitive or personal experience of students' achievements?

Interpretive Questions
Where are we strong relative to expectations?
Where are we weak relative to expectations?
What may be some of the underlying causes?
What are some emerging themes in all this information?
Which of these is most important for you? Why?
Which of these needs to be dealt with first? Why?

Decisional Questions
From the standpoint of building on our strengths and dealing with weaknesses, what subjects or areas of skill do you hear the group saying are the highest priorities for improvement in our school?
Which do you hear the group saying are the lowest priorities at this time?
What three or four of these high priority areas do we most need to focus on improving in the next few years?
Who will work on the plans (and the actions) for each priority?

Evaluating School Achievement Data (continued)

Watch the flow of answers very closely. The very first time someone answers a question that has not been asked yet, ask them to hold that response until the question where it will be most appropriate. If you have written the questions on the board as an agenda, it will be easier. Do it gently, but nipping the tendency to jump ahead in the bud seems important in this conversation. More than three or four priority subjects or areas for school improvement is probably not manageable.

This conversation is the first step, and can be followed with an action plan for each priority.

Closing

This is tremendous work, and will make a difference in our students' performance. We will take a couple of weeks for each group to complete an action plan, and then have another quick meeting to share the plans.

Improving Parent/Teacher Conferences

Designed for
Teachers and Staff Members

Situation
The principal and teachers are evaluating the parent-teacher conferences at a staff meeting.

Rational Aim
To extract what staff has learned from talking to parents at the conferences.

Experiential Aim
To affirm the experience of the conferences.

Hints
Be sure to get out objective information from all or many of the teachers before moving to more depth.

The Conversation

Opening
Our parent-teacher conferences for this grading period have come and gone. Let's take a few minutes to reflect on the experience, and think about what we learned from talking with the parents.

Objective Questions
Let's go around the room, so each teacher can respond to the first three questions.
How many parents came?
How many students came?
What percentage of your students' parents came?
What specific comments or questions do you remember?

Reflective Questions
What pleases you most about what you heard?
What concerns you?

Interpretive Questions
What common patterns are you hearing from across the school?
Do you see any really outstanding concerns that need to be addressed immediately?
What can we learn from these interviews?
What implications might this have for us?

Decisional Questions
What actions do we need to take in the next grading period?

Closing
Thank you for your insight. Now for the next agenda item.

Reflecting Informally on a Leadership Program

Designed for
Teachers and Staff Members

Situation
A group of teachers from across a district has partici- pated in a project on facilita- tive leadership. They have come together to celebrate what's working and plan for the next year. They start with individual worksheets.

Rational Aim
To evaluate the facilitative leadership program and extract their learnings.

Experiential Aim
To experience affirmation for the whole year's efforts — setbacks as well as accom- plishments.

Hints
This conversation works well as a large group process. It can be done first as individu- als writing answers on a work- sheet, then sharing answers to each question around a table of five or six people: each table group choosing a few key answers to share with the whole group.

The Conversation

Opening
The purpose of this exercise is to give us an opportunity, as leaders, to reflect on our work this past year and to share our reflections. There are no right or wrong answers. Listen actively and appreciatively. The hope is that we will learn something by listening to one another's experiences. Take some time to answer the questions on the worksheet for yourself. We will be sharing answers as tables, but it is up to each individual to decide what is appropriate for you to share.

Objective Questions
In which projects and activities this year did you or a colleague provide leadership for improved student learning?

Reflective Questions
Which projects and activities are you are most proud of?
What stories or vivid memories out of this year give a human face to your work?

Interpretive Questions
Which of these stories give meaning or insight to your work — for example, how student success happened, results were achieved, or obstacles overcome?
What tools, techniques and approaches have worked for you, or have been key to our leadership this year?
What are things you did that have *not* worked, things that you would do differently or advise against?
What have you learned about leadership in the past year?
What new insights will you apply in the coming year? How?

Decisional Questions
What do you need to do to complete and document the accomplishments of this year?
Who or what needs to be celebrated, recognized, or thanked?

Closing
Thank you for your insights.

Evaluating the Implementation of a New Curriculum

Designed for
Teachers and Staff Members

Situation
A new provincial math curriculum was introduced a year ago. Teachers are reflecting on their learnings about its implementation, so that they can ensure improved student learning.

Rational Aim
To understand the effects of implementing the new curriculum.
To create consensus on directions for further growth.

Experiential Aim
To increase teachers' confidence in their ability to use the curriculum effectively to meet student needs.

The Conversation

Opening
We need to take some time to evaluate the new math curriculum.

Objective Questions
How has the math program changed since the arrival of the new curriculum last year?
What do you do differently now?
What changes have you noted in the students' knowledge, skills, and attitudes?

Reflective Questions
What changes are you most comfortable with?
What changes make you feel uncomfortable?
What changes have been most easy for students to adjust to? Most difficult?

Interpretive Questions
How has student learning improved?
Are there areas where you are less than satisfied?
What key strands and expectations do we need to focus on to continue to improve student learning?
What areas need the most attention at this point?
What resources are still needed to implement the curriculum successfully?
What in-service training do we still need to implement the new curriculum to improve student learning?

Decisional Questions
What are some reasonable steps that we can take now to keep us moving in the right direction?

Closing
I think these steps will continue to improve our student's learning. Thank you for your thoughtfulness and care.

Processing a Training Session Quickly

Designed for
Teachers and Staff Members

Situation
At the end of a training session, participants hold a quick conversation to process their experience. They have about 15 minutes.

Rational Aim
To recall ideas and concepts presented and relate them to their own lives.

Experiential Aim
To be ready to apply learnings.

The Conversation

Opening
Let's do a quick look back at this session to process it.

Objective Questions
What ideas, concepts, tools, or techniques were identified in this session?

Reflective Questions
What excited you about the material in the session?
What frustrated you?

Interpretive Questions
How do these ideas and concepts relate to your professional experience?
What significance do they have for you?

Decisional Questions
What will you do with this information?

Closing
It's been a great day. See you tomorrow.

Debriefing the Day

Designed for
Teachers and Staff Members

Situation
A team of teachers sits down together after a day of team teaching. They are focused on what students need.

Rational Aim
To review the significant events of the day and to plan for tomorrow.
To foster shared learning and reflective practice.

Experiential Aim
To generate team enthusiasm about working together and improving teaching practice.

Hints
This type of conversation replaces complaints and off-hand comments with a shared process of learning from both positive and negative experiences.
For a quicker conversation on subsequent days, ask only the most pertinent questions, or substitute others. Keep the conversation short and to the point to avoid burnout.

The Conversation

Opening
Visualize what occurred today, from the time the bus delivered our students, until a moment ago when the last student left.

Objective Questions
What is one scene, conversation, phrase, or sound, which stands out to you as you review the day?
As you reflect on the day, who is one student who stands out in your mind?
What is one role you played today?

Reflective Questions
At what point today did you have a strong feeling about what was going on?
When did you see students particularly engaged? Particularly disconnected?
What in this experience reminds you of students you've worked with in the past?
Where did you feel the most success in the classroom?

Interpretive Questions
What did we do today that best reflects powerful learning principles?
If you were a student in this class, what would you tell your family about what you learned today?
What insights have we gained about the students in our class and how our teaching affects them?
In which areas did we work most effectively together? Where do we need to improve?

Decisional Questions
What did we do today that we want to continue doing tomorrow?
Which students, if any, need special help tomorrow? How will we provide it?
How can we work together more effectively to address student needs?
What is one accomplishment we each plan to achieve tomorrow?

Evaluating a Project Group's Work

Designed for
Teachers and Staff Members

Situation
A group of teachers in a new school has been studying the possibility of organizing the school into multi-age groupings. As they have been working, the educational climate has been changing, and their energy has been flagging.

Rational Aim
To explore some of the issues and opportunities the group currently faces, and decide where to go next.

Experiential Aim
To struggle with the paradox of conflicting agendas and directions.

The Conversation

Opening
We've been working with the concept of multi-age groupings and there seems to be some concern about its real benefits. There are concerns about the potential for achieving such a change in the conflicting agendas of the current educational climate as well as the demands of putting the idea into practice. It seems that we need to come to an understanding as to where this group is headed so we can move forward with a common purpose.

Objective Questions
What do you remember about our meetings over the past few months?
What decisions do you recall us making?
What products have we produced for ourselves so far?
What changes have you observed since we began?

Reflective Questions
What has been the most frustrating or worrisome part of this group's work?
What excites you about what we're doing?

Interpretive Questions
What else have we learned about the tasks we've set out for ourselves or the way we work together?
How would you describe the dilemmas we face as a group?
What are the areas where we are seeing the greatest creativity – most positive impact?

Decisional Questions
What is our highest priority at this point in time?
What shall we do at this point?

Closing
How would you summarize this discussion?

Reflecting on a Personal Growth Plan with a Mentor

Designed for
Teachers and Staff Members

Situation
A school system encourages teachers to form mentoring relationships with other teachers. Each teacher makes "growth plans" for their own learning and reflects on them with a coach. A coach asks the following questions to help the teacher assess the past year and plan the future.

Rational Aim
To evaluate the past year, and plan the next year

Experiential Aim
To affirm the past and have the courage to continue

Hints
It is helpful to have an outside coach to ask these questions, but it can also be done as a solitary exercise. If the coach has been there all year, she can give her responses as well to many of these questions. For example, the mentor might say, "It seems to me that..." in answer to some of the questions, after giving time to the protégé to answer first.

The Conversation

Opening
Let's take a few minutes to evaluate last year and begin a plan for the next year.

Objective Questions
What have been some key events this year in terms of your growth plan?
What projects did you work on?
What other events do you remember — important conversations or discussions or decisions made?

Reflective Questions
What accomplishments are you most proud of?
Where did you have the most difficulty?
What surprised you?

Interpretive Questions
What would you say is your most important accomplishment this year related to your growth plan?
How will your experiences of this year and your reflections affect what you do in the coming year?
What are your hopes and dreams?
What are your more concrete goals for the coming year?
Where might you encounter difficulties in moving towards your goals?
Who could be of assistance to you in achieving your goals?

Decisional Questions
What will you do differently next year?
What are your next steps?

Closing
I'll leave you to do your detailed action plan.

Evaluating a Difficult Teaching Situation Alone

Designed for
Teachers and Staff Members

Situation
A university professor has experienced a frustrating semester, where several students have been highly critical of his lectures. He decides to do a personal reflection.

Rational Aim
To have a clearer plan of action.

Experiential Aim
To feel motivated to teach next semester.

Hints
As in most internal conversations, especially on intense subjects, it is hard to stay focused. The key is not the precise questions, but to guide the levels of thinking in a disciplined way, with one student after another.

The Conversation

Opening
OK, let me reflect on my own situation, so I can arrive at a clearer plan of action and feel motivated to attempt it (as against ducking the whole thing).

Objective Questions
What do I remember about interactions with student X *(choosing one of the students)*?

Reflective Questions
What has been most difficult for me?

Interpretive Questions
What would I say are the underlying issues?

Decisional Questions
What can I do to work more effectively with this student?
What is the first action I need to take?

Planning for a Special Education Student

Designed for
Parents and Community

Situation
The school has placed John in a special education program. At the end of each year the teacher, other staff, and parents review the students' progress, and plan the next year. The team leader leads this conversation.

Rational Aim
To discern two or three academic and social needs to focus on for this student for the next year.

Experiential Aim
To develop a trusting relationship between parents and the teacher.

The Conversation

Opening
We're here for the annual review of John's progress. Let's start with a recap of last year's accomplishments.

Objective Questions
What were some of John's accomplishments last year?

Reflective Questions
In which courses was he less successful than desired?
What were the courses John did well in?
When did you notice John getting enthusiastic?
What were high points?
When did you notice John was discouraged?
What were low points?
What was the most difficult issue to deal with? For his teachers? For his parents? For John?

Interpretive Questions
What are some of the factors that seem to be leading to these frustrations?
What can be done to ease your anxieties?
How are John's needs changing as we look forward to next year?

Decisional Questions
What could we do differently next year?
What areas will we focus on?
What academic courses should John take?
What can we do to ensure John has a successful year?

Closing
I'm confident we will make this a very good year for John.

Talking with a Teacher at a Parent/Teacher Conference

Designed for
Parents and Community

Situation
A parent is talking with the teacher at the parent-teacher interview, and wants to get the most information possible from the teacher in the allotted time.

Rational Aim
To find out from the teacher how her child is doing academically.
To find out the teacher's recommendations.

Experiential Aim
To have the teacher experience affirmation of parental support.

The Conversation

Opening
I need to get a clear picture of my child's academic performance.

Objective Questions
What information can you give me on how she is doing? Marks? Portfolio? Journals and Workbooks?
This is what I have observed….

Reflective Questions
What are you pleased with as the teacher?
What are you worried about as the teacher?

Interpretive Questions
How does this performance measure up to class standards?
What are the challenges she is struggling with?

Decisional Questions
What do we need to do to support her performance?
When should we talk next?

Closing
Thank you. I'll do my part to work with you and support her learning.

Talking with a Parent at a Parent / Teacher Conference

Designed for
Parents and Community

Situation
A teacher uses this format to have a quick but thoughtful conversation with each parent on parent-teacher interview night.

Rational Aim
To share information on student performance.

Experiential Aim
To establish mutual respect and trust, and commitment to supporting the student's best learning.

Hints
This structure can also be used alone by the teacher to prepare for the interview.
The teacher also answers the questions in this conversation. A challenge in using this conversation is in keeping the questions and the teacher's own answers separate.
Having the questions on a sheet that the parent can see will help make the process more objective for all participants.
The teacher may want to prepare a couple of "if – then" streams at the interpretive level. These would likely arise out of the discussion on strengths and weaknesses. I.e. if the student is performing very well in all areas, the questions would be related to deepening the challenges and exploring other learning options. If there are specific concerns, they need to be followed up with questions that are relevant to those specific concerns.
(continued)

The Conversation

Opening
Hi, I'm Johnny's teacher. I'm glad to meet you. Let's look at some information on your son's progress this term.

Objective Questions
Here is some data from my gradebook on attendance and performance.
What clarification do you need about this information?
What would you add to these reports from what you have seen?

Reflective Questions
What pleases you most about how Johnny is doing?
What worries you?

Interpretive Questions
Where are Johnny's strengths in this area?
What are his weaknesses?
What might be underlying reasons for this level of achievement?
What are the major opportunities or concerns we need to address?
What implications does this have? For the teacher? For the parent(s)? – For the student? For others in the system?

Decisional Questions
What can we do to support and encourage Johnny's highest possible achievement?

Closing
Thank you very much. With both of us working together to support Johnny, he'll do well.

Talking with a Parent at a Parent / Teacher Conference (continued)

For instance, the student may understand math processes, but doesn't do the calculations right and gets confused. The student doesn't seem to be able to read at the expected level or speed. The student isn't attending regularly. If there are deep concerns about the overall performance, the conversation will be somewhat different.

Discussing a Portfolio with Parents and Teacher — Led by Student

Designed for
Parents and Community

Situation
Students at a high school keep portfolios on their course work, so that they can report to parents and teachers on their progress. In this session, the student shows her work, and facilitates a conversation on it.

Rational Aim
To have the student, parents and teachers understand the student's performance and progress.

Experiential Aim:
To have the student experience pride and ownership of her learning journey.

Hints
This conversation can also be used in primary school, adapting the questions to a simpler form, but keeping the four levels.

The Conversation

Opening
I'd like to share samples of some of the work I have done over the past six months.

Objective Questions
As you look through my portfolio, what do you notice?
What catches your eye — assignments, projects, layout, signs of progress, something unusual etc.?

Reflective Questions
What about my portfolio of work excites you?
What worries or concerns you?

Interpretive Questions
What do you understand now about my progress from these work samples?
What questions do you have for me or my teachers?
What achievements do you see?
What, if any, gaps do you see in my learning?
What things do you think that I have to work on?

Decisional Questions
What do you suggest may be the next steps?
What support do you think I need?
What do we need to do to make sure these things happen?

Closing
Thanks for participating. It'll be great to work on this together. Let's go!

Deciding about Retaining a Student in a Grade

Designed for
Parents and Community

Situation
Toward the end of the year, despite the hard work of parent and teacher, a child is not performing well enough for the next grade level. The teacher asks for the parent to talk with her about whether the student should repeat the grade.

Rational Aim
To decide whether a student should be retained in the same grade or not.

Experiential Aim
To engage parents and teachers (and the student as appropriate) in serious dialogue about the student's progression.

Hints
The conversation can be adapted to having a parent lead the conversation with the teacher or the principal.

The Conversation

Opening
As you know, I am really concerned about Fiona's learning, and I have been considering whether to have her repeat this grade. I would like to talk through this with you, to get your thoughts.

Objective Questions
What are some of the areas that you have noticed Fiona achieving in lately?
What is she not achieving in lately?
What is she enjoying most at home and at school?

Reflective Questions
What concerns do you have about Fiona's learning progress?
These are some of my concerns and those of Fiona's other teachers. What is your reaction to these?
What are you satisfied with in her progress?

Interpretive Questions
If Fiona were to repeat a grade, what would be some of your concerns and questions?
What would be some of the pros and cons of retaining her in this grade?
What do you see as the learning needs of your child?

Decisional Questions
How do feel we can best support these needs?
How would we sum up where we are on all this?
Are we ready to make a decision, or do we need to explore this further?

Closing
Thank you very much for your concern. It's clear we all want Fiona to succeed.

CHAPTER 10

Creative Applications

Chapters 6 to 9 focus on templates for single conversations that can be adapted to a variety of situations. In the editing process, they were streamlined so that they could be adapted easily to many similar situations.

The examples in this chapter are so unique that they could not fit the pattern of the rest of the book. They are included because they can spark your creativity and insight in applying the four levels of the Focused Conversation method in a wide variety of school situations.

Often focused conversations are not stand-alone events. They may be used in sequence and in combination with other methods and tools to enhance learning or consensus. Three examples in this chapter demonstrate linked conversations that follow each other, or work with other tools of participation in creative ways.

As well, beyond the strict definition of a conversation, the four levels of the reflective process can also used for presentations, surveys, note-taking, and lesson planning, among other things. It is helpful to see how the thinking structure can be used in this way, so that we can discern when it is appropriate to have a conversation, and when it is helpful to use the four-level pattern in another way.

Since understanding of some of these creative applications is enhanced by the specific locations or cultural settings for which they were designed, I have included those locations in this chapter where possible.

Conversations Linked in a Curriculum Stream

Drug Education Curriculum for Grade Four Students

Overall Situation

A fourth grade teacher in New Jersey requested the community health nurse to add art and focused conversations to a packaged drug education curriculum. This curriculum includes seven conversations that were used at various points during a year with the same group of students.

The topics of the conversations include:

• Healthy Behavior: Taking Care of Ourselves
• Conversations on a movie—*Lots of Kids Like Us* —before the movie, right after the movie, the next day
• After another movie on how to keep friends, have fun, and stay out of trouble
• After an exercise on refusing drugs after a role play
• At the end of the project on celebrating community

Healthy Behavior: Taking Care of Ourselves

Designed for
Students – Elementary

Situation
This conversation was used as an introduction to the curriculum.

Rational Aim
To raise consciousness about healthy behavior.

Experiential Aim
To experience the topic of healthy behavior as fun and interesting.

The Conversation

Opening
Let's stand in a circle, and go around it once, each giving an answer.

Objective Questions
What is your name?

Reflective Questions
What is your favourite food? Your favourite color?
What is something you love to do?

Interpretive Questions
What is something you do that is not so healthy for you?
What is one way you keep yourself healthy?
How do you take care of yourself?

Decisional Activity
Now let's return to our seats. Here are some markers and paper for you to use. One piece of paper has a large circle on it.
Draw pictures of ways to take care of yourself in the large circle on the piece of paper.
When you are finished, I want each of you to hold up your art work and say something about it.
We are going to make a book of all of your work.
What name shall we give to this book you've just created?

Closing
We will create a poster together using your art work, and telephone numbers to use in emergency situations as well as telephone numbers for support people and support groups, to hang for the year in the classroom. We will also put each student's art work as a page in a laminated book, which will remain in the classroom library for the school year.

Conversation on the Movie, *Lots of Kids Like Us,* Before the Movie

Situation
A month later, prior to viewing the video *Lots of Kids Like Us*, the following conversation is held.

Rational Aim
To focus attention on the topic of alcoholism and its effects. To be prepared to understand the video.

Experiential Aim
To be prepared to deal with the impact of the video.

The Conversation

Objective Questions
When I say the word *alcoholism*, what comes to mind?
What other words do people use to describe someone who drinks a lot?

Reflective Questions
Where have you seen alcohol being used? In movies or television? In real life?

Interpretive Questions
What effects does alcohol have on the person drinking?
On families? On other people?
Why is it important to talk about these things?

Decisional Questions
Keep these things in mind as we watch this movie.

Conversation on the Movie Right After the Movie

Situation
The video is shown.

Rational aim
To comprehend the effect of alcoholism on kids.
To be aware of some skills of coping with problems of alcoholism.

Experiential Aim
To personally empathize with the effects of alcoholism.

The Conversation

Opening
Let's all spend a few moments in silence, reflecting on our feelings and where we can identify with one of the characters.
Here is an 81/2"x 11" paper with a large circle drawn on it. First you can write the answers to the following questions on the back of the paper, if you like. At the end of the conversation, you will be asked to draw something on the circle.

Objective Questions
What words, images, or sounds did you notice in the video?

Reflective Questions
What feelings did you see in the characters?
What part made you want to cry?
What part made you afraid?
What part made you feel lonely or really alone?
What other feelings did you experience?

Interpretive Questions
Where did you see kids using skills to cope, respond to, or deal with their situations in the video?
What are the coping skills you find useful in your life?

Decisional Questions
Turn the paper over and draw what you feel about this. Select colors you feel drawn to, and create art work within the circle that answers this question: What has happened to you as a result of seeing this video?

Conversation on the Movie the Day after Viewing the Movie

Rational Aim
To enable students to articulate their learning from the movie.
To have some idea of where to go for help when affected by alcohol.

Experiential Aim
To care about the effects of alcoholism and know that others care.

The Conversation

Opening
Let's look back at the film we saw yesterday. Sometimes it's easier when we have had a little time to think about it.

Objective Questions
What do you remember today that was in the film?

Reflective Questions
What did you feel while you were watching the video?
What scene or part of the video made you feel like that?
What were you reminded of in your own life?

Interpretive Questions
What was this film about for you?
What did you learn from this film?

Decisional Questions
What can you do to get help when you are in a situation like this?

Closing
You have created your own mandalas as you drew your pictures in the circles yesterday. We will laminate these and return them to each of you for use as a personal place mat to keep in your own desk or to take home.

Keeping Friends and Having Fun while Staying out of Trouble

Situation
Students see a video on trouble situations where drugs or alcohol are made available to students, and different ways that they refuse them. The students brainstorm trouble situations that they might encounter, then work on refusal skills. These skills are modeled and practiced, then role-played by the students. After the role-plays, the entire class engages in the following reflective questions.

Rational Aim
To be able to use different refusal skills appropriately in real life.

Experiential Aim
To be committed to refusing drugs and alcohol.

The Conversation

Opening
Wow, this was a busy day. Let's see if we can remember all that we did.

Objective Questions
What activities did we do today?

Reflective Questions
How did it feel to role-play?

Interpretive Questions
What did you learn from the role-play you were in?
What did you learn from another role-play?
What difference do these skills make in your life?

Decisional Questions
What shall we put on posters to remind us of these skills?
How will you personally remember these skills?
How will you use them?

Closing
Saying no when it is necessary is not easy, but I am confident that you will be able to do it. You are strong, and now you are skilled.

Celebrating Community

Situation

This final session with the class focuses on their life together as a class. They review and reflect upon their experiences of being a community, to close the year's curriculum.

Rational Aim

To provide an opportunity to reflect on personal growth and learning about taking care of ourselves.
To connect class learning with everyday life.

Experiential Aim

To be aware of personal changes and learnings.
To have the capacity to take new awareness into daily life and make wise choices.

The Conversation

Opening

We have had a very interesting year together as a community of people in this classroom. As a class, you are a supportive community and can help each other to take care of yourselves. Let's reflect on the year from this perspective.

Objective Questions

What are words and pictures around the room which remind you of this community?

Reflective Questions

What were your feelings in the beginning of the year as you got to know each other?
How do you feel different now?

Interpretive Questions

What does learning all about healthy people, coping, and refusal skills have to do with *taking care of ourselves*?

Decisional Questions

What does your art work tell you about yourself?
What will you do to take care of yourself now, after all we've learned here?

Closing

Let's stand in a circle and thank one another for being the supportive community we are for one another. Your teacher is there for you, and will give help and feedback to you. As a class, you are a supportive community and can help each other to take care of yourselves.

Conversations Linked with Other Tools

Nunavut Inuuqatigiit Leadership Workshop

Situation

This event, which includes a series of conversations and workshops, was designed to be done with Inuit school leaders from across the new territory of Nunavut. All participants speak one or more Inuit languages as well as English.

The first day focused on culturally appropriate learning, and the next several days focused on school leadership.

Successful Learning in a Culturally Appropriate Way

Rational Objective
To have a deepened understanding of one's own personal learning styles and learning patterns common to Inuit culture.

Experiential Aim
To gain strength & confidence as an Inuit learner.

The Conversation

Opening
Welcome and context.

- Introductions exercise: Let's star by each choosing a partner. With your partner, share your name, where you're from, your birthday, and an event where you really learned something.

- Write both your names on small cards.

- Introduce your partner to the whole group and put their name on the wall map with a string linking it to this place.

- Facilitator puts up some working assumptions (i.e. Everyone has wisdom. We need everyone's wisdom for the wisest result. There are no wrong answers. The whole is greater than the sum of its parts. Everyone will hear others and be heard.)

- Facilitator tells a personal story of learning outside a school, such as learning how to make cookies from grandmother.

- Facilitator talks through the questions, which have been written on a flipchart or on a paper copied for each small group.

- Break into small groups. "We are going to have this conversation in small groups. Please speak in any language you are comfortable speaking in the small groups."

Conversation on Learning in Small Groups

Rational Objective
To have a deepened understanding of one's own personal learning styles and learning patterns common to Inuit culture

Experiential Aim
To gain strength & confidence as an Inuit learner

The Conversation

Opening
In a minute we will split up into small groups to talk about our learning experiences. Please talk in any language you are comfortable with. Answer the following questions and bring back some stories, common elements, and underlying factors to share with the whole group.

Objective Questions
What are some events/times when you really learned something? Or you observed learning?
These may be outside school, inside school, or a traditional skill.
What did you learn?
How did you learn?
Who/what was the teacher if there was one?

Reflective Questions
What parts of these sound like the most fun?
What parts sound difficult, painful or boring?

Interpretive Questions
What are common elements of successful learning in your stories?
Summarize these common elements, and write them down.

Decisional Questions
What are the underlying factors that make learning successful for you? List them.
These ideas might help you think of underlying factors:
    A quiet environment? Noisy?
    Moving around? Still?
    Being alone? With others?
    Visual images? Lots of words? Sounds or talking?
    Others?

Closing
It's time to take our work back to the whole group.

Whole Group Reflection on Reports and Conversation on Learning

Rational Objective
To have a deepened understanding of one's own personal learning styles and learning patterns common to Inuit culture.

Experiential Aim
To gain strength & confidence as an Inuit learner.

The Conversation

Opening
Each team reports uninterrupted.
Reports: Each group shares their stories, common elements of successful learning and really important underlying factors in successful learning.

Objective Questions
What words caught your attention as you heard these reports?

Reflective Questions
What made you laugh?
Where did you think, "Oh, yeah, I understand that!"
What images came to mind?

Interpretive Questions
What patterns did you hear? — Where did you hear more than one group say the same thing?
Which factors are the most important? Which were said the most times?
Drawing together what you've heard, what elements are there when successful learning is going on? *(Write on flipchart.)*

Decisional Questions
Imagine that academic learning and cultural learning are in two separate boxes.
Drop the boxes, leaving two piles of kinds of learning. Now move the piles of learning together.
What might all that we've learned here mean for learning and for a school based on Innuqatigiit, or Inuit cultural learning (i.e. geometry out on the land, or teamwork in solving problems)?
This conversation is followed by a consensus workshop *(see the Appendix for procedures)* with the focus question "What do we want to see in a place of learning (school) that supports successful Inuit culturally appropriate learning?"

Leadership Conversations

Rational Objective
To have a deep understanding of leadership that works in this culture.

Experiential Aim
To gain hope that leadership is possible, and to have a glimpse of selves as leaders.

The Conversation

Opening
First let's reflect for a moment on our experience of yesterday's work on successful learning:
What do you recall from yesterday? *(Objective)*
Where did you have an "Aha!"? *(Reflective)*
What is one thing you learned yesterday that is useful to you? *(Interpretive)*
What is your commitment to successful learning? *(Decisional)*

Opening
Let's step back a bit: When I say the word *Leadership:*...

Objective Questions
What's the first image that comes to mind?

Reflective Questions
What's your gut level reaction?

Interpretive Questions
What are some of the things that real leaders do?
What responsibilities do leaders have?

Decisional Questions
Summarize what we've said — what do leaders do?

Conversations on Leadership in Small Groups

Rational Objective
To have a deep understanding of leadership that works in this culture.

Experiential Aim
To gain hope that leadership is possible, and to have a glimpse of selves as leaders.

The Conversation

Opening
Now let's have conversations in small groups again.
At the end of the conversation, bring back qualities of successful leadership to share with the whole group.

Objective Questions
Each person tells a story.
What are some times you've seen real leadership going on?
In the camp?
In the community?
In the school?

Reflective Questions
What do you like most about being a leader?
What is difficult about being a leader?
What kinds of leadership make you uncomfortable?

Interpretive Questions
What common elements are there in your stories?
What are some of the qualities of successful leadership?

Decisional Questions
How would you summarize the qualities we have discovered?

Reflections on Reports and Conversation on Leadership with the Whole Group

Rational Objective
To have a deep understanding of leadership that works in this culture

Experiential Aim
To gain hope that leadership is possible, and to have a glimpse of selves as leaders

Hints
Sometimes conversations that follow each other directly do not have a separate closing. The closing of one conversation and the opening statement of the next may be the same sentence.
Procedures for the *consensus workshop* method referred to here can be found in the Appendix.

Other Applications
Reflecting on how we learn does not have to be in a culturally specific context. Sometimes we get caught up in traditional expectations of teaching others, without reflecting on our experience of successful learning. One or two of these conversations might be an interesting way to start a year, or to introduce an inservice session on learning styles.

The Conversation

Opening
We want to hear reports now from each group, including a story and a summary of the qualities of successful leadership you identified. Let's hear one report after the other, without any interruption.

Objective Questions
As you heard these reports, what words caught your attention?

Reflective Questions
What was really exciting?
What were you reminded of by someone else's report?

Interpretive Questions
Which of the qualities you heard would you pick out as key qualities of leadership in Inuit culture?

Decisional Questions
What might this mean for leadership in a place of learning (school) based on Inuuqatigiit?
This conversation is then followed by three consensus workshops:
    A vision for leadership in schools (places of learning),
    Obstacles to that vision, and
    Strategies to deal with the obstacles and realize the vision.

Debriefing a Cross-Cultural Simulation Game

Situation

Students in a university class in Japan are preparing for a trip abroad. They start with a cross-cultural simulation game called *BaFá-BaFá*, created by Simulation Training Systems. This is a powerful game, and a lengthy debriefing discussion is essential to processing emotions and sharing insights.

Whole Group Debriefing Discussion

Rational Aim

To show that language is not the only way of communication.
To understand hidden dimensions of culture.
To prepare participants to meet people of other cultures and backgrounds.
To be able to compare cultures for similarities and differences.

Existential Aim

To experience culture shock and express feelings about it.
To appreciate different values in other cultures.

Hints

The first two levels can be conducted immediately after the game and the second two levels could be done a week later, after the journal writing. Total time required is 60 to 90 minutes.

The Conversation

Opening

Let's stand back from this experience for a little while and debrief our experience.

Objective Questions

Ask Beta persons: What did you see in the Alpha culture? What were they doing?
Ask Alpha persons: What did you see in the Beta culture? What were they doing?
To Beta persons: What do you think were the rules of the Alpha culture?
To Alpha persons: Is that right? What were the rules of your culture?
To Alpha persons: What do you think were the rules of the Beta culture?
To Beta persons: Is that right? What were the rules of the Beta culture?
What did the anthropologists (first observers) report in their analysis? What did they miss?
What did you try to do when you first entered the other culture? What happened when you tried that?

Reflective Questions

How did you feel when you first visited the other culture?
How did you feel when you came back from the other culture?
How did you feel about the visitors from the other culture? How did you interact with them?
When your nose was painted or you were pushed by someone, how did you feel?
What part did you enjoy the most? Where did you have fun?

(continued)

Whole Group Debriefing Discussion *(continued)*

What part was most difficult or confusing?

How do you feel about your own culture (Alpha or Beta)?

Interpretive Questions

Which country would you like to live in? Why?

What are some of the values of the Alpha culture? The Beta culture?

What did you discover about yourself?

What did you find out about intercultural communication?

Decisional Questions

How will this experience affect you when you travel abroad?

How will this affect the way you communicate with visitors here in Hokkaido?

If you do your visit over again, what would you do differently this time?

Closing

Reflection Papers:

Following the group discussion, participants are asked to write a reflection on their experience in their journals. A short form for a few paragraphs of writing and a long form of several pages have been designed. The students are asked to be conscious of their own changes that occurred during and after the game.

The following is a list of the interpretive level questions used for the short homework assignment: Write one paragraph about the following questions:

What did you know about yourself that you didn't know before the game?

What did you learn about intercultural communication that you didn't know before?

How do you think this knowledge or experience will help you in the future?

Journal Writing after the Experience of the Simulation Game

Situation
Participants are given a written assignment to reflect on their experience after a cross-cultural simulation game.

Rational Aim
To probe the experience of a cross-cultural simulation game.
To be more aware of personal values.

Experiential Aim
To wrestle with unexpressed values.

Hints
The simulation game can be done in about 90 minutes followed by 45-60 minutes of discussion. If done over several days, an extended three-session schedule can be done.

The Conversation

Opening
Write four to six pages of your reflections in a journal during the next week concerning the *BaFá-BaFá* simulation game. Here are some questions to answer in your writing.

Objective Questions
• Recall: What happened?
• What did you see?

Reflective Questions
• How did you feel during the simulation? When did you feel that?
• When did you feel confused?

Interpretive Questions
• What did you learn about visiting another culture?
• What did you learn about yourself?
• What did you learn about intercultural communication that you didn't know before?

Decisional Questions
• How do you think this knowledge or experience will help in the future?

Closing
Write a poem or draw a picture that describes your experience of the whole game.

Complex Use of the Four Steps

Discussing an Incident in a Justice Circle Conferencing Process

Situation

In New South Wales, Australia, an urban public school with a large Aboriginal and multi-cultural population has been working with the police to develop restorative justice processes. These justice circles allow students to deal with minor and major offences, involving their families, friends, and others in the process of conflict resolution, healing and behavioral change.

Formal Justice Circle Conferencing Process

Rational Aim
To bring healing and closure to harm caused in the school setting

Experiential Aim
To have all concerned in a specific incident own the behavior, experience the pain caused, and have the possibility of making restitution and moving on.

Hints
Note that each "party" is asked objective, reflective, and interpretive questions before the conversation moves to the next person. The decisional level is asked to both victim and offender at the same time. These levels are indicated with O,R,I, and D before the questions. Involvement in the process pre-supposes a willingness on the part of all participants to attend, and that the offender has admitted his/her actions. Participants may include supporters of both victim and offender (e.g., parents, fellow student/s, relevant school staff, a community person/friend, where appropri-

The Conversation

Opening
Welcome.
Introduce each participant and their relationship to the victim and offender.
We want to explore in what way people have been affected, and how we can work towards healing the harm that has been done.

1.Facilitator to Offender/s:
O - Can you tell us what happened, and how you came to be involved?
R - What were you thinking about when this happened?
R - What have you thought about since?
I - Who was affected? How?
(Be sure offender owns the action) This may require some follow through with other objective questions to get an appropriate level of detail.

2. Facilitator to Victim/s:
O - Can you tell us what happened? Again this may require some follow through with other objective questions to get an appropriate level of detail.
R - How did you feel at the time?
R - How did you feel afterwards?
I - How has this incident affected you? What has been hard for you?
I - What did your friends/family think?

(continued)

Formal Justice Circle Conferencing Process *(continued)*

ate). Numbers should be kept to a minimum, and include only people key to the restitution process for the young people concerned.

This formal process may take one to three hours. It should be emphasized that it is important to take the necessary time to work through the issues with the students involved.

Other Applications

This can be used in other community settings where punitive justice may be seen to be counterproductive. Often when an offender is able to take in the impact of their behavior, that behavior may change.

3.Facilitator to Victim's supporters:
O - What did you hear about this?
R - How did you feel? What has been the hardest thing for you?
I - What has happened since?
I - What are the main issues for you?

4. Facilitator to Offender's Supporters:
O - What did you hear about this?
R - How did you feel? What has been the hardest thing or you?
I - What has happened since?
I - What are the main issues for you?

5. Facilitator to Offender:
You've heard from *(victim)* and *(supporters and/or family)*.
I - Is there anything you want to say?

6. Agreement — Facilitator to victim and then to victim supporters:
D - What would you like to see happen out of this?
(Allow discussion time about possible reparation) There may need to be some guiding questions here.

Facilitator to offender:
D - Is there anything you want to say to… (victim?)
D - Is there anything you should do to make things right?
D - What do you think about what victim & supporters have said? How is it fair?

Facilitator to offender's supporters, and then to all:
D - How is this fair?
D - What is our agreement about how we will close this?

Closing

It is important that we clarify what has been agreed here….
(Repeat agreement for confirmation. Invite any other comments where appropriate. Thank participants and invite to stay for refreshments. Informal time is important.)

Informal Version of the Justice Process

The Conversation

Objective Questions
• What happened?

Reflective Questions
• What were you thinking about at the time?
• Who has been affected?
• How were they affected?

Interpretive Questions
• What's been the hardest thing for you?
• What have you thought about since?

Decisional
• What needs to happen now?

Closing
Thank you for your thoughtfulness and willingness to solve this. Let's go do it. More — acknowledgement, thanks, etc.

Unusual Applications of the Four Levels of the Process

Conversation on a Web Site for Students

Situation

After the first election in Nunavut, the new Inuit territory of Canada, a newspaper ran an article about the election. Elementary students were asked to discuss the conversation on a website, accessible to students in schools across the territory of Nunavut.

Other Applications

Of course the questions in this conversation can be done live in class on news articles, as well.

A News Article on the Nunavut Election

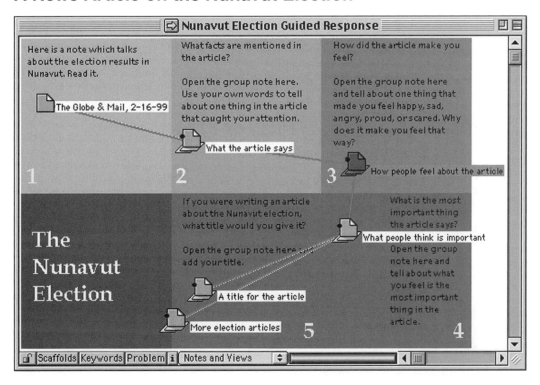

Four-Level Procedures for Interviewing Students to Resolve a Schoolyard Fight

Situation

In a school in New Jersey, a teacher brings in to the principal two kids who've been fighting. They stand in front of the desk - both are talking at once or sulking. The principal is not purely asking questions: she is directing students.

Rational Aim

Solve the problem, and learn how to avoid the problem the next time.

Experiential Aim

To experience being heard, and accept responsibility for solving the problem.

Hints

At the end of the reflective level, invariably one holds out his hand for a handshake. Stop them, explaining that the other may not be ready to shake now, or even at the end of the conversation. The transformation may begin to occur after the second level of reflection because they each have a gut experience of being listened to and heard.

The Conversation

Opening

Quietly ask them to face each other.

Objective Level

Gently ask A on the right to tell B his version of what happened. Tell B he will then have his turn and ask him to simply listen to A without arguing or asking questions.

After B has had his turn, A gets another turn, a chance to add as much as he wants while B continues to listen silently.

Then B adds more if he wishes.

Reflective Level

Still facing each other. This time B gets to start:
How did/do you feel about this?
Back and forth, each in turn until they have no more to add, while the principal and the other listen silently.

Interpretive Level

What have you learned from what happened? Back and forth again. A starts.

Decisional Level

Still facing each other. B starts. What could you do the next time you're in a situation like this?

Closing

I'm really proud of you for listening to each other and learning from this experience. You are responsible students. Let's go now, and have fun.

Using the Four Steps in a Presentation:
A Directive by a Principal on an Urgent Issue

Situation
An urgent situation around custody of a student has arisen requiring an exception to school policy. Parts of this are confidential, as sharing them could expose the school to legal liability if made public, but a child's safety is at stake.

Rational Aim
To ensure staff will understand the reasoning behind the principal's decision, and the decision itself.

Experiential Aim
To ensure staff will trust the decision and carry it out.

Hints
This is not a focused conversation. It is a speech by the principal, when he/she has had to make a decision and tell their staff. The principal has used the conversation structure to think through the decision, and also uses it to communicate.

Other Applications
Other topics that are not up for discussion may be presented in this way. It will communicate that the topic has been clearly thought through.

The Conversation

Opening
The principal calls all the staff to the staff room just before school for a five-minute announcement.

Objective Level
Our school policy is that a parent who has custody of a child may sign a release from allowing someone else to pick up their child from school. Johnny's mother has signed one to allow his uncle to pick him and his sisters up. Johnny has just come crying to school and told me some confidential information.

Reflective Level
I am very upset by what I have heard.

Interpretive Level
In my analysis of the situation, Johnny's and his sisters' safety may be at stake if they go with their uncle today after school.

Decisional Level
No one is to allow Johnny or his sisters to go with his uncle, either during the day, or after school. I want to know immediately if the uncle or anyone comes looking for them today. If there is any question, bring them personally to my office. I will be trying to contact Johnny's mother.

Closing
Does everyone understand this? Will you all operate out of what I am asking?
There's the bell. I'll see you later.

Using the Four Levels as a Format for a Report Form: Simple Team Report

Situation
When a team is unable to come together for regular progress reports, this "conversation" can be sent out as a form to be filled in — it can even be e-mailed.

Rational Aim
To evaluate the work of the past year.
To share learnings and determine future challenges.

Experiential Aim
To experience affirmation of progress and learning.

Hints
Each of these reports can be sent to everyone else on the team, or they can be compiled into one and sent out. They can be used as the basis for a group conversation. The form guides each person to think more deeply about their experience. It also helps the reports to be parallel, so that they can be collated or compared more easily.

Other Applications
Questions like this can be put on an interactive website or a list serve for the whole group to respond to.

The Conversation

Opening
Please use these questions to evaluate the work of the team.

Objective Questions
What have been key results and outcomes of our past work? Give some examples as evidence of these key results and outcomes.

Reflective Questions
What's worked?
What did not work?

Interpretive Questions
What are some important learnings from what we have done?
What are some challenges facing us?

Decisional Questions
What implications do you see for this year, and beyond this year?
What will it take to overcome these challenges?

Closing
Please return your answers as soon as possible so they can be collated with those from other members of the team.

Focused Conversation Embedded in an Icebreaker: Team-building Process

Situation

A school team in Arizona does an exercise to get to know each other at the beginning of the year. The exercise starts with a video on teamwork. Then each person is given a page with a drawing of a compass with lines to put a person's name at each of the four points of North, South, East and West.

Rational Aim

To process a video on teamwork.

Experiential Aim

To break the ice and meet a number of new people.

Hints

You may want to put the four steps of the message on a chart.

The worksheet is complex, but it provides a tool for making sure people talk to more than one person.

The Conversation

Opening

Let's use this drawing of a compass with others' names to mix us up and process our learnings from the video. Each person finds four people that they don't know well, and each puts their name at one of the corners of the compass for the other.

Objective Questions

(NORTH Partner = WHAT or FACTS — Discuss facts only here, not feeling.)

Find your NORTH partner (the person whose name is on your compass at the North point), then look at me please. With your NORTH partner, discuss WHAT you remember from the video. Discuss FACTS:

What words do you remember?

What pictures can you recall?

(Give 1-2 minutes for partner discussion, then pull group back together with signal — hand raised or other signal. Ask for a few volunteers to share some facts with the group.)

Reflective Questions

(SOUTH partner = GUT or REACTIONS)

Thank your NORTH partner and find your SOUTH partner, then look at me please.

With your SOUTH partner, discuss the GUT or REACTIONS you had watching the video.

How did you feel during the video?

Where were your feelings most uplifted? Most anxious? Most challenged?

(Give 1-2 minutes for partner discussion, then pull group back together with signal — hand raised or other signal. Ask for a few volunteers to share some reactions with the group.)

Interpretive Questions

(EAST partner = SO WHAT, or IMPLICATIONS)

Thank your SOUTH partner, find your EAST partner, then look at me please *(wait)*.

We've shared WHAT or facts and GUT or REACTIONS. Now we'll discuss a bit more deeply the SO WHAT, or IMPLICATIONS.

What are the implications of what we just viewed for our school?

(continued)

Focused Conversation Embedded in an Icebreaker: Team-building Process
(continued)

How are we as a team, often similar to what we just viewed?
(Discuss in pairs — volunteers then share with group.)

Decisional Questions
(WEST partner = NOW WHAT or ACTIONS)
Thank your EAST partner. Now find your WEST partner. Look at me please.
We've shared WHAT or facts, GUT or reactions, SO WHAT or implications:
Now we'll focus on NOW WHAT or actions.
What actions do we need to take to foster teamwork?
What steps can we take to support teamwork?
(Discuss in pairs — volunteers then share with group.)

Closing
Thank your WEST partner and return to your original seat.
The dialogue technique we've just used is called the Focused Conversation Method.
Four parts are necessary for rich, meaningful discussion:

     O....objective or FACTS......................WHAT
     R....reflective or REACTIONS.............GUT
     I ....interpretive or IMPLICATIONS....SO WHAT
     D....decisional or ACTIONS.................NOW WHAT

Using the Four-Level Process on an Evaluation Form: Strategic Planning Process Evaluation and Feedback Form

Situation
A facilitator has just led a school in a participatory strategic planning process. He hands out a quick feedback form with questions and spaces to write answers.

Rational Aim
To have solid, thought-through feedback on the process.

Experiential Aim
To enable participants to experience their wisdom and journey affirmed.

Hints
This makes a good generic evaluation form for training and participatory events. Be sure to leave enough room for writing answers.

Other Applications
For a training event, the last questions can be "How will you apply the process?" and "What further training are you interested in?"
This can also be held as a conversation to wrap up a day.

The Conversation

Opening

Could you please take a minute to fill out this form before you leave the room?

Objective Questions
What were two or three key events of this process for you?

Reflective Questions
What were high points?
What were low points?

Interpretive Questions
What were important accomplishments and/or information?
Please complete this statement in a sentence or two: The significance of this process for me has been....
Rate this process on a scale of 1 to 10, with 10 being the highest. Circle one.

Decisional Questions
What suggestions do you have to improve this process?
Looking to the next year or two, what suggestions do you have for how we evaluate and measure the effectiveness of the plans we have decided on?

Closing
Thank you. Please leave on the table for the facilitator to pick up.

Using the Four-Level Process on a Survey Form: Survey on the Implementation of a New Statewide Initiative

Situation
Teachers are being introduced to a new statewide initiative for assessment. They have used the initiative for a year. The following conversation is sent to teachers as a survey to reflect on and return to the administration.

Rational Aim
To have data on how the assessment initiative is working in the individual classroom.

Experiential Aim
To have a sense of being valued and heard.

Other Applications
Although this is written as a survey to be filled out by individuals, the same questions could be used in focus groups or in school staff conversations, or with parent groups.

The Conversation

Opening
This survey is on the implementation of the assessment initiative. Please take twenty minutes to go through these questions and give your honest responses. We will use your thoughts to improve the initiative.

Objective Questions
What assessment activities have you done in your class in the past year?
What interventions have you done in your class in the past year?

Reflective Questions
As you have conducted assessment and interventions in your class what has surprised you? What worried you?
What pleased you?

Interpretive Questions
How has your use of the assessment and intervention initiative affected the ability of your students to achieve the state standards in your class?
What are the weaknesses of the assessment and intervention initiative in your grade level?
What are its strengths?

Decisional Questions
What are your next steps in using the assessment and intervention strategies in your class?
What recommendations would you make to administration, based on your experience?

Closing
Please return this survey to administration.

Telephone Notepad Form

Data/facts

Reactions

Significance

Action

Part III

Appendices

Contributors

The following people contributed conversations to this book. Their wisdom, insight, and creativity are a valuable gift to education.

Doug Balsden, Cochrane, Alberta
Karen Wright Bueno, Thornton, Colorado
Gail Burton, Calgary, Alberta
Lucille Chagnon, Willingboro, New Jersey
David Church, Winnipeg, Manitoba
Burna and David Dunn, Denver, Colorado
Carol Fleishman, New Orleans, Louisiana
Karen Greenham, London, Ontario
Pearl Gregor, Edmonton, Alberta
Trish Griffin, Winnipeg, Manitoba
Beret Griffith, San Carlo, California
Barbara Hall, Yellowknife, Northwest Territories
Gordon Heaton, Highlands Ranch, Colorado
Don Hinkelman, Hokkaido, Japan
Ellen Howie, Altamont, New York
Robyn Hutchinson, Lewisham, Australia

Suzanne Jackson, Toronto, Ontario

Sorene Kampen, Dawson Creek, British Colombia

Simon Koolwijk and Jouwert van Geene, Amsterdam, The Netherlands

Leslie Lambie, Dawson Creek, BC

Teresa Lingafelter, Redlands, California

Barb Low, Woodstock, Ontario

Sandy McAuley, Yellowknife, Northwest Territories

Jann McGuire, Lindsay, California

Dana McTavish, Winnipeg, Manitoba

Barb MacKay, Winnipeg, Manitoba

Jill Persichetti, Houston, Texas

Claudette Petuin, Winnipeg, Manitoba

Linda Reid, London, Ontario

Jim Roscoe, Shanghai, China

Pam Santesteban, Glendale, Arizona

Pat Scheid, Washington, DC

OliveAnn Slotta, Denver, Colorado

Brenda Hutcheson Smith, Nome, Alaska

Cathryn Smith, Winnipeg, Manitoba

Jim Spee, Redlands, California

Peter Taylor, Boston, Massachusetts

Kathy Thomas, London, Ontario

Karen Snyder Troxel, Chicago,

Jane Stallman, San Francisco, California

Jeanette Stanfield, Toronto, Ontario

Jeff Steckley, Woodstock, Ontario

Brenda Turnbull, Woodstock, Ontario

Carol Webb, Denver, Colorado

Jim Weigel, Phoenix, Arizona

Judi White, Crescent City, Florida

Creating a Culture of Change Project, Ontario Teacher's Federation, Ontario

Parents, teachers, and students from the public and separate school boards in
Durham Region, Ontario

Teachers from Manley, Mason, Herzl, Lawndale, Dvorak, Lathrop, Pope, Johnson,
and Chalmers schools in Chicago, Illinois

Possible Starting Points for Using the Focused Conversation Method

One crucial key to the success of a focused conversation is to start with a concrete object or shared experience. This allows the conversation to start with objectivity. Sometimes finding the appropriate starting point is as difficult as creating appropriate questions. This list of possible starting points may help.

Film and Video	**Documents or Papers**
training videos	policy documents
feature films	mission statement
special scenes or sequences that capture a valued insight	survey results
	written assignments
music videos	project description

Art and Art Forms

posters

charts

paintings

photos and photo books

sculpture

music

dance

Learning Experiences

demonstration of a concept

demonstration of a skill

student projects

role plays

speeches or presentations

Current events

Magazine article

Newspaper article

Television documentary

Personal Experiences

field trip

vacations

games

stories of previous experience, shared
    in the opening of the conversation

a walk around the space to be discussed

Professional Experiences

staff evaluations

parent visit

student interview

recent staff meeting

playground conflict incident

Well-known Characters

heroes or famous persons

great teachers

villains

mythological characters

characters from literature

sports or movie stars

Myths and Stories

folk tales

legends

myths

nursery rhymes

Literature

plays

short stories

plays

writings

children's stories

Quotes

professional literature

cultural texts

inspirational texts

Symbols

the Earthrise

cultural symbols

Sample Questions for Each Level of the Conversation Method

These questions represent a range of possible questions at each level of the conversation method, drawn from various conversations in this book. They are listed here to give you ideas and challenge your imagination as you create a conversation from scratch.

Objective Questions

1. Who were the characters in this story?
2. What objects did you see?
3. What does the document say?
4. What vehicles were in the accident?
5. What words did the teacher say?
6. Describe what you see on your desk.
7. What are some of the program concerns that your staff members have expressed?
8. What steps did we go through? First? Second? Next?
9. What were the main points made by the speaker?
10. What body language did you notice of each team?
11. What are questions of clarity you have?
12. Read the survey summary aloud.

13. What words or phrases catch your attention?
14. Think back over your life and share one experience that you've had searching for information.
15. As you flip though this, what are the sections of this curriculum?
16. What facts catch your attention here?
17. What other information do you know?
18. What background data do we know?
19. What comments have you heard from parents?
20. What has happened since the last time we met? (Accomplishments, events, activities related to our task).
21. What statistics do we know about our own district?
22. What behaviors were observed or reported regarding this teacher?
23. Where have you seen effective teams working? Give an example.
24. What is one thing you heard the speaker say?
25. Imagine you were a video camera on the wall. What actions, words, phrases, objects, scenes are recorded on your tape?
26. What specific acts of misbehavior have you seen?
27. When have you caught him behaving well?
28. Tell me what has been happening. Try to do this from the standpoint of an external reporter, holding a video recorder. Be as specific as you can.
29. What did you do today? Show me some things you did today.
30. What are the rules?
31. Which parts of the program do you remember most?
32. What is one evaluation and/or assessment strategy that you use in your classroom?
33. What data catches your eye?
34. What topics did we cover?
35. As you look through my portfolio, what do you notice? What catches your eye?

Reflective Questions

1. What part of the story did you laugh at?
2. When were you afraid or experience terror?
3. What was confusing, exciting, or overwhelming today?
4. What have you been grateful to someone else for during this year?
5. What were the high points for some of you? What were lows?
6. What images jump to mind?
7. With whom did you first identify?
8. What am I interested in that this reminds me of?

9. What surprises you?
10. What memories did this bring out?
11. When did you want to cheer?
12. When did you really "get into it"?
13. Where did you get caught up in this video?
14. Where were you irritated or angry?
15. What was your favorite animal?
16. What's your first reaction?
17. What concerns you about the implementation of our plan?
18. What is still inspiring?
19. Which ones made the hair on your neck rise, or pointed to a vulnerability?
20. What part - word or phrase - of this strikes you as the most powerful?
21. What parts of this are most alarming?
22. What parts are you okay with?
23. Stand in a parent's shoes. What is frustrating for him/her?
24. Which part did you really hate?
25. What about our work do you feel best about?
26. Where did we struggle the most?
27. What animal or geometric shape comes to mind?
28. What part of the work ahead seems like a heavy burden?
29. What did your face look like? Make a face like that.
30. What's the worst part of this for you?
31. What are the biggest joys of teaching for you? The biggest challenges?
32. What shocked you about this?
33. What made you want to escape?
34. What is one thing that someone has done that makes you mad?
35. What parts were the tiniest bit hopeful or a little fun?
36. What worries you the most about his behavior?
37. Where in your body did you feel your frustration?
38. What do you like to do here? Bring me your favourite thing to do.
39. When do you feel sad, angry, or unhappy here?
40. What did you feel the most proud of? What do you wish you had done better?
41. What surprises were in the program for you?
42. Where have you had a big "aha!" happen?
43. What part put me on the edge of my chair?
44. What part put me to sleep?
45. What stories or vivid memories out of this year give a human face to your work?

Interpretive Questions

1. What was the story about? What was the message of the story?
2. What is a key insight you had?
3. Where did you have a breakthrough?
4. How will it affect you? Your work?
5. What's been most worthwhile?
6. What's been least helpful?
7. What was the most outrageous thing he did to allow/encourage learning?
8. Why did the accident happen?
9. What might I learn from this?
10. What did you discover about yourself?
11. If you were in this story, who would you be? Why?
12. Why is this important?
13. What will be the greatest challenge to you in applying this process?
14. How are these issues similar or connected?
15. What seems most "on target" about what they are doing there in relation to our school's needs and objectives?
16. How is this similar to the equation we did last class? How is it different?
17. What are common elements in your stories of successful learning?
18. What were some unique elements?
19. What patterns did you hear - where more than one group said the same thing?
20. What is it you think the author was trying to get across to the readers?
21. What makes that an important message?
22. How were you changed by this experience?
23. In which areas did we work most effectively together? Where do we need to improve?
24. What is a value that comes form your observations and reflections?
25. Which of these issues concern you the most?
26. What would you have done differently?
27. If you were in this picture, who would you be and what would you be doing?
28. Where did you have problems? Why?
29. What are some alternatives to this draft?
30. Which of the recommendations are most important for you? Why?
31. Which parts are most critical to complete?
32. Which of the questions, concerns, objections or obstacles that you have heard so far is going to require the most careful response?
33. What was missing from this session for you?
34. What trends are emerging?

35. What do these look like in real life, in our day-to-day operations?
36. What does this reveal about who we are?
37. What are some ways we can organize these concepts to teach them effectively?
38. What are some of the root issues?
39. What do you perceive to be the possible implications of this new situation, both positive and negative? Why?
40. What might this look like when we're done?
41. What are some things we could do to deal with this?
42. What does that indicate or tell you about our work of the last year?
43. What is one new idea you learned?
44. How does it relate to your role in the school, jurisdiction or school council?
45. What are its strengths and weaknesses?
46. What have you heard the group saying are some common goals we have?
47. Which of these common goals is your first priority?
48. What lessons can we learn from this study?
49. What are some values in our society that foster sexual harassment?
50. Why do you think this problem occurred?
51. What are you discovering?
52. What might we do if our own children were watching and learning from this example?
53. What are the positive and negative implications of possible decisions?
54. What are the long term and short term benefits of the possible decisions, and how do they compare?
55. What else we could do that would accomplish the positive intent and minimize the negative impacts?
56. What are the key differences between the old and the new requirements?
57. What parts of this are workable? Non-workable?
58. What is the purpose of this?
59. How could the this help make our school more effective?
60. How does this impact students?
61. What impact does teamwork have on instruction?
62. What do you think is at the bottom of this?
63. What values do we want to see in our new leadership?
64. What seem to be critical factors in dealing with student conduct effectively?
65. How are you different now?
66. How might we be different a year from now?
67. In the big picture of things, what is the importance of today?
68. Which behaviors have the most negative impact for Johnny and for other students?

69. What may be some of the causes of this behavior?
70. What implications – both positive and negative - does this have for students?
71. For staff?
72. For the school system?
73. What are the values behind this decision?
74. What story would you tell us about this?
75. What are some of our core values?
76. How would we talk about our sense of purpose?
77. How could you have handled this differently?
78. What is something you've learned to do here? – Point to it.
79. What skills did you learn here that will help you in the future?
80. What would you tell other students they would learn if they applied to get into the program?
81. What does this look like in the classroom?
82. What are some similarities you noticed among the methods? Differences?
83. What are some emerging themes in all this information? *(Write on board.)*
84. What patterns are you hearing here across the school?
85. What is most relevant and important for my teaching situation?
86. What was I most challenged by?
87. What tools, techniques and approaches have worked for you, been helpful, have been key to our leadership this year?
88. What are things you did that have *not* worked, things that you would *do differently* (or tell others not to do)?
89. Do you see any gaps in my learning?
90. What do you understand now about my work & progress from these work samples?
91. What would be some of the pros & con's of repeating?
92. What do you see as the learning needs of your child?
93. What areas need the most attention at this point?
94. What resources are still needed?

Decisional Questions

1. How would you summarize what you have learned from this version of the story?
2. What are practical applications that come to mind?
3. How would you name the whole?
4. If you had to explain to somebody from "outer space" what you did today, what would you say?
5. Draw a picture about this.
6. What do we need to do over next few months?

7. Who will take on which tasks?
8. What recommendations do you have?
9. What do I do to carry out this assignment?
10. If you do your visit over again, what would you do differently this time?
11. How do you think this knowledge or experience will help in the future?
12. Who needs to be involved?
13. How will you start?
14. Based on what we've seen to date, what can we set as learning objectives for the end of next week?
15. What do you need to do to master this process?
16. Summarize the underlying factors.
17. How do we implement our learnings?
18. How has this story changed you, or your thinking?
19. What are you willing to commit to?
20. What can we call this exercise?
21. How would you summarize the meaning of this painting for today's world?
22. How will the response be organized?
23. How can we support each other?
24. What is one thing you'll do as follow-up at your school?
25. Who will take responsibility for any of these changes?
26. What do we want to suggest to the writing team?
27. What are our next steps? Who will do them?
28. What are all the things we have to do to get this done? (Write them on sticky notes.)
29. Name the year, maybe with a piece of poetry or a visual image.
30. If you had 2 minutes to explain SBDM policy to someone else who was not in this session, what would you say?
31. What is the first action you have planned in your project?
32. What else can we do to assist you?
33. What can we do to prevent harassment from happening?
34. What are the appropriate consequences to these problems?
35. How can we clear this up?
36. How shall we communicate our decision to the rest of the parents, staff, and students?
37. How can we put these elements together to create a solution we can live with?
38. What will these things cost?
39. How will we pay for them?
40. Who will make sure these things happen?

41. What strategies can be applied?
42. How can we integrate these critical factors into our school yard routines?
43. What can we do to prevent this from happening again?
44. What can we do to care for each other?
45. What choices will you make?
46. What metaphor would sum up this day?
47. When shall we come back and evaluate what's working, and regroup?
48. What might we do to limit his destructive behavior and encourage his positive behavior?
49. What can we do to affect this decision?
50. What can we do to cope with this new situation – to minimize negative impacts and strengthen or create positive impacts?
51. What is the first action we need to take?
52. Where would you like to use this information?
53. What can be done to influence good behavior?
54. Draw me a picture of the best part of preschool. Tell me about your picture.
55. What changes would you recommend?
56. What skill or other learning have you developed that you will use in your regular class work?
57. Who will you go to if you need more help?
58. What are three or four high priority subjects or strands that we most need to focus on for improvement in the next few years?
59. What actions do we need to take in the next grading period?
60. What areas will we focus on?
61. What will I share with my colleagues?
62. Who/what needs to be celebrated, recognized, reinforced, rewarded, thanked?
63. What do we need to do to make sure that this happens?
64. How will your experiences of this year and your reflections affect what you do in the coming year?

ToP™ Consensus Workshop Method

The ToP™ Consensus Workshop Method helps bring individual ideas on a topic into group consensus. This method can be used for planning, model building and problem solving. It can be done in 1 to 3 hours.

Preparing

In preparing for this type of workshop it is important to establish

The Rational Aim - the product, result, decision or understanding that will be the outcome of the workshop. The aim indicates the kind of result rather than the specific content.

The Experiential Aim - the experience you want the group to have in the workshop or how you want the people to be different as a result of their participation.

The Focus Question - an open ended question that names the topic, clarifies the time frame under consideration and enables the group to focus on the intended result. The focus question triggers the brainstorm, provides a guide for grouping the data, and focuses the naming of the resulting groupings.

Steps in the Group Process

There are 5 major steps in the ToP Workshop Method.

Setting the Context - Setting the Stage

Brainstorming Ideas - Generating New Ideas

Grouping the Ideas - Forming New Relationships

Naming the Clusters - Discerning the Consensus

Reflecting on the Session - Confirming the Resolve

Setting the Context - Setting the Stage

Provide the group with a context for their work.

- Clarify the reason for holding this workshop. History, purpose etc.
- Explain the expected product or outcome
- Outline the process, the timelines and participation guidelines
- Highlight the focus question

Brainstorming Ideas - Generating New Ideas

Brainstorm 35 to 60 ideas in response to the focus question.

- Brainstorm responses individually and select "best" ideas from the list.
- Brainstorm ideas in small groups. (Aim for about 50 ideas from the whole group. (Divide 50 by the number of small groups to get the number of ideas per group.)
- In small groups, write each idea on a 5" x 8"card in big, bold letters.

Grouping the Ideas - Forming New Relationships

Group the ideas into clusters with similar responses to the focus question.

- Gather ideas from each group. Read each card aloud for the group and stick the cards on the wall with sticky-tack or masking tape. As you put the cards on the wall, let the participants know that they can ask questions of clarity. If an idea is not understood, ask the group that generated the idea to briefly explain it. Do this process in "rounds." In the first round, ask each group for the 2 clearest ideas. In round 2 ask for the 2 strongest ideas.
- Find 5 - 6 pairs of ideas that answer the focus question in a similar way. Move these cards together and add a neutral symbol, like a circle, that the group can use as a reference. You are creating columns or clusters of cards.
- Ask the group for ideas that are different from those currently on the wall. Put them up – reading each one as you do.
- Continue developing clusters of related ideas. Place all of the ideas into clusters.

Naming the Clusters - Discerning the Consensus

Name each cluster with a title that reveals the group's answer to the focus question.

- Read the items in a cluster.
- Ask the group for key words on the cards.
- Discuss the cluster to clarify the main idea in relation to the focus question.
- Name the cluster with a short "title" that holds the insights and group's consensus. The title will be an answer to the focus question.
- Repeat for each cluster.

Reflecting on the Session - Confirming the Resolve

Enable the group to reflect on their experience and their consensus.

- Rearrange the clusters to create a "chart" that holds the total picture and the relationships among the clusters.
- Use the Focused Conversation method to bring the workshop to closure. (Striking ideas, surprises, new ideas, major insights and consensus.)
- Identify the next steps to be taken. (What, who, when, how?)

APPENDIX 5

ORID Rap

Created by a group of facilitators who had recently learned the Focused Conversation method, this rap is an unusual way to communicate the steps the method.

> Yo! You're lookin' for participation
> Gettin' folks to talk without hesitation
> Tune in dudes to what we say
> 'Bout the methods of the ICA!
>
> First, you ask what's happenin' now.
> What's the jive? What's the wow?
> If you get facts in the conversation
> You've got the step called observation.
>
> Now all that data ain't near enough
> You've got to get into the feelin' stuff
> What's the notion behind the emotion?
> Reflection questions will make it spoken.

This facilitation has got you yearnin'
To figure out what they've been learnin'
If you wanna sound like an ICA native
Gotta ask a question that's interpretative.

What's this mean that we should do
What's for me and what's for you?
Ask some questions with great precision
And you will get a group decision.

O - R - I - D it'll make consensus
Defuse tension, bring down fences
So join with your sisters and your brothers
Now you know how to facilitate others

APPENDIX 6

Focused Conversation Method Flow

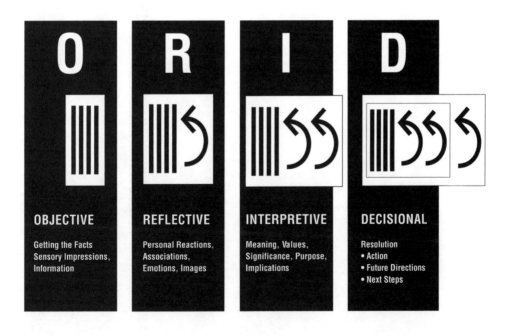

O OBJECTIVE — Getting the Facts Sensory Impressions, Information

R REFLECTIVE — Personal Reactions, Associations, Emotions, Images

I INTERPRETIVE — Meaning, Values, Significance, Purpose, Implications

D DECISIONAL — Resolution
• Action
• Future Directions
• Next Steps

FOCUSED CONVERSATION METHOD FORM

TOPIC:

OPENING	RATIONAL AIM (S)		EXPERIENTIAL AIM (S)	CLOSING
	OBJECTIVE	REFLECTIVE	INTERPRETIVE	DECISIONAL

Bibliography

Ada, Alma Flor, and María del Pilar de Olave, *Hagamos Caminos, Exploramos, Teacher's Edition*, World Language Division, Addison-Wesley, Menlo Park, CA, 1986

BaFá- BaFá, a simulation game from Simulation Training Systems, P.O. Box 910, Del Mar CA 92014, sts@cts.com, website: www.stsintl.com/schools/bafa.html

Bloom, Benjamin, *Taxonomy of Educational Objectives*, David MacKay, New York, 1956

Boulding, Kenneth E., *The Image: Knowledge in Life and Society*, University of Michigan Press, Ann Arbor, 1956

Bruner, Jerome, *The Culture of Education*, Harvard University Press, Cambridge, Mass, 1996

Chagnon, Lucille, *Voice Hidden, Voice Heard: A Reading and Writing Anthology*, Kendall-Hunt, Davenport, IA 1998

Clark, Barbara, *Optimizing Learning: The Integrative Education Model in the Classroom*, Merrill Publishing, Columbus, OH, 1986

Dewey, John, *Art as Experience*, Minton, Balch and Co., New York, 1934

Dickinson, Dee, *New Developments in Cognitive Research,* New Horizons for Learning, Seattle, 1987

Drath, Wilfred H. and Charles J. Palus, *Making Common Sense: Leadership as Meaning-making in a Community of Practice*, Center for Creative Leadership, Greensboro, North Carolina, 1994

Gardner, Howard, *Frames of Mind: The Theory of Multiple Intelligences*, Harper and Row, New York, 1983

Goleman, Daniel P., *Emotional Intelligence*, Bantam, New York, 1995

Guild, Pat Burke and Stephen Garger, *Marching to Different Drummers*, Association for Supervision and Curriculum Developments, Alexandria, VA, 1985

Hutchinson, Robyn, *Family Youth Conferencing Process* — developed with Restorative Justice Unit, NSW Police for teacher/student use, Lewisham, Australia, 2000

ICA CentrepointS: "The Art Form Method" on Golden Pathways CD-ROM, Chicago, 1996

Institute of Cultural Affairs, Imaginal Training Methods, *Image: A Journal on the Human Factor*, Volume XI, Chicago, 1981

Institute of Cultural Affairs, *Fifth City Preschool Education Manual*, Chicago, 1981

Jenkins, John, *International Facilitator's Companion*, DigiTALL, Groningen, The Netherlands, 1997

Johnson, D., R. Johnson, and E. J. Holubec, *Cooperation in the Classroom*, Interaction Book Company, Edina, MN, 1988

Kierkegaard, Søren, *Despair: The Sickness Unto Death*, Princeton University Press, Princeton, NJ, 1980

Kloepfer, John, "The Art of Formative Questioning, A Way to Foster Self-Disclosure", in *Group Facilitation: A Research and Applications Journal*, International Association of Facilitators, Winter, 1999 Volume 1, Number 1

Kolb, David, *Learning Style Inventory*, McBer and Co., Boston, 1976

Kolb, David, *Experiential Learning: Experiences as the Source of Learning and Development*, McBer and Co., Boston, 1984

Langer, Susan, *Reflections on Art*, Arno Press, New York, 1979

Lazear, David, *Seven Ways of Knowing: Teaching for Multiple Intelligences*, IRI Skylight, Palatine, IL, 1991

Lazear, David, *Seven Ways of Teaching: The Artistry of Teaching with Multiple Intelligences*, IRI Skylight, Palatine, IL, 1991

McCarthy, Bernice, *The 4MAT System: Teaching to Learning Styles with Right/Left Mode Techniques*, EXCEL Inc., Barrington, IL, 1980

McCarthy, Bernice, "What 4MAT Training Teaches Us about Staff Development", in *Educational Leadership* 42, 7 (April 1985)

Perkins, David, *Smart Schools: Better Thinking and Learning for Every Child*, Free Press, New York, 1992

Piaget, Jean, *The Construction of Reality in the Child*, Basic Books, New York, 1954

Piaget, Jean, *The Psychology of Intelligence*, Littlefield Adams, Totowa, NJ, 1972

Seagren, Ronnie, "Imaginal Education", in *Approaches that Work in Rural Development*, Volume 3, K.G. Saur, Munchen, 1988

Saul, John Ralston: from an address to the graduating class of the University of Western Ontario, Spring 1999, as quoted by Robert J. Giroux, "The Need for Long-Term Thinking and Support" in *Education Canada*, Fall 1999, Vol. 39, No. 3

Schein, Edgar, *Organizational Culture and Leadership* (2nd ed.), Jossey-Bass, San Francisco, 1992

Slotta, OliveAnn, editor, *Imaginal Education Workbook*, Institute of Cultural Affairs, Denver, CO, 1996

Spencer, Laura, *Winning Through Participation*, Kendall/Hunt, Davenport, IA, 1992

Stanfield, R. Brian, editor, *The Art of Focused Conversation: 100 Ways to Access Group Wisdom in the Workplace*, ICA Canada and New Society Publishers, Toronto, 1997

Williams, R. Bruce, *Twelve Roles of Facilitators for School Change*, IRI Skylight, Arlington Heights, Illinois, 1997

Williams, R. Bruce, *More than 50 Ways to Build Team Consensus*, IRI Skylight, Arlington Heights, Illinois, 1993

Index

The Institute of Cultural Affairs

The Canadian Institute of Cultural Affairs, a non-profit organization, builds people's capacity for shared social responsibility by researching, publishing, teaching and demonstrating participatory approaches to learning, leadership, planning and action. As of January 2001, ICA Canada celebrated its 25th anniversary.

ICA internationally is a global non profit social change organization that has existed for 45years. Today it operates in over 32 countries on six continents.

The current scope of ICA's activities in Canada is in sharing experience & knowledge in social capacity building methods through:
- Publishing; newsletters, periodicals, manuals and books
- Research on social innovations, needs, trends & models
- Education & learning: conferences, forums and study groups
- Projects in individual and community development & leadership

In October of 1999 ICA Associates Inc. was created as a for-profit organization to distribute ICA Canada's knowledge through publications, training courses and facilitation consultation.

Other Resources Available From The Canadian Institute of Cultural Affairs and ICA Associates Inc.

The Art of Focused Conversation: 100 Ways to Access Group Wisdom In The Workplace by R. Brian Stanfield. - 222 pages

The Courage To Lead: Transform Self, Transform Society by R. Brian Stanfield. This book challenges us to take charge of our own internal quest for meaning in life. It encourages us to move out of paralysis by acting powerfully wherever we are. - 260 pages

Courses Specifically for Educators:

Group Facilitation for Educators. Two days that provide two invaluable methods for involving staff, students, and parents in planning and making decisions.

Focused Conversation for Educators. A one-day course that provides experiential learning and guided practical application of the Focused Conversation method for success. Based on the book.

School Improvement Action Planning. This one-day course is designed for school administrators and facilitators. Step-by-step procedures provide tools to involve stakeholders in evaluating school assessment data and creating prioritized plans for school improvement.

Other facilitation and training can be tailored to specific needs.

How To Contact Us

By mail: The Canadian Institute of Cultural Affairs
579 Kingston Rd
Toronto Ont.
Canada M4E 1R3

By telephone: 416-691-2316
Toll Free (outside of Toronto and in Canada) 877-691-1422
By fax: 416-691-2491
By e-mail: ica@icacan.ca
Web site: www.icacan.ca

Books to Build A New Society

New Society Publishers' mission
is to publish books that contribute in fundamental ways
to building an ecologically sustainable and just society,
and to do so with the least possible impact on the environment
in a manner that models that vision.

If you have enjoyed *The Art of Focused Conversation for Schools*,
you may also want to check out our other titles
in the following categories:

Progressive Leadership
Ecological Design & Planning
Environment & Justice
New Forestry
Accountable Economics
Conscientious Commerce
Resistance & Community
Educational & Parenting Resources

For a full list of NSP's titles,
please call 1-800-567-6772,
or check out our web site at:
www.newsociety.com

NEW SOCIETY PUBLISHERS